The
Sporting
Spaniel
Handbook

Loren Spiotta-DiMare

With Color Photography
Drawings by Michele Earle-Bridges

Dedication

To my husband, Lou DiMare, who shares my love for animals, and to our spaniels, Chelsea and Smokey, who delight and inspire me every day.

With special thanks to two wonderful friends and fellow dog lovers, Eleanor Semanchik and Ilyse Rothstein.

SF429
.S7
S655
1999

All inquiries should be addressed to:
Barron's Educational Series, Inc.
250 Wireless Boulevard
Hauppauge, New York 11788
http://www.barronseduc.com

Library of Congress Catalog Card No. 99-31699

International Standard Book No. 0-7641-0884-0

Library of Congress Cataloging-in-Publication Data
Spiotta-DiMare, Loren.
    The sporting spaniel handbook / Loren Spiotta-DiMare.
        p. cm.
    Includes bibliographical references.
    ISBN 0-7641-0884-0 (alk. paper)
    1. Spaniels. 2. Dog breeds. 3. Hunting dogs. I. Title.
    SF429.S7S655   1999
    636.752'4—dc21   99-31699
                                                                    CIP

Printed in Hong Kong

9 8 7 6 5 4 3 2 1

Photo Credits

Loren Spiotta-DiMare: pages vii, 96, 126, 130; Nance Photography: pages viii, 136 top right, 137 top; Judith E. Strom: pages 2, 3, 10, 12, 13, 15–19, 28, 30, 31, 33 top, 35, 47, 48, 55, 59, 68, 79, 81, 82 top, 84, 92, 94, 95, 97, 98, 106, 116, 117, 119–121, 127, 129, 131, 136 top left, 138 bottom; Tara Darling: pages 4, 9, 11, 33 bottom, 42, 44, 45, 57, 58, 70, 80, 93, 104, 105, 107–109, 111, 122, 136 bottom, 138 top left, 140; Kent and Donna Dannen: pages 5, 6, 8, 14, 22, 23, 25, 29, 34, 36, 43, 54, 56, 61, 69, 71–73, 82 bottom, 83, 118, 137 bottom, 138 top right; Pets by Paulette: page 7; Norvia Behling: pages 21, 24; Beth Marley: pages 27, 128, 132.

Cover Photos

Front: Tara Darling, Beth Marley, Judith E. Strom; Inside Front: Animals Animals; Inside Back: Kent and Donna Dannen; Back: Kent and Donna Dannen, Judith E. Strom.

About the Author

A life-long animal lover, and member of the Dog Writers' Association of America, Loren Spiotta-DiMare has been writing about animals, dogs in particular, for over twenty years. She has a special affinity for the sporting breeds. This is her fifth book.

Loren lives in rural northwestern New Jersey where her own spaniels thoroughly enjoy the country life.

Important Note
This book has been written to offer a comparative guide to the nine spaniel breeds recognized by the American Kennel Club in the Sporting Group. Breed chapters describe personality traits, habits, aptitude for training, grooming needs, and exercise requirements. Every effort has been made to provide accurate, up-to-date information about spaniels raised by reputable breeders, that is dogs of sound physical health and good character.

Contents

Preface

I've always been enamored with the sporting breeds, especially spaniels. There's something innately appealing about their soulful eyes, floppy ears, soft fur, and stubby little tails. Water spaniels have their own delightfully unique characteristics with their curly coats and longer tails. Add to that their sweet, fun-loving, and loyal temperaments and you have, at least to me, the epitome of what a dog should be.

I'm not sure which traits attract an individual dog owner to a certain breed or breeds. But I distinctly remember the first time I fell in love with mine. As a teenager, I was attending a local obedience club with a mixed-breed when my eyes fell upon a striking red and white spaniel speckled with freckles. He was a Welsh Springer Spaniel and surely the most beautiful dog I had ever seen.

Years later when I was in a position to buy my first purebred dog, I happened on another Welsh Springer Spaniel at an outdoor dog show. It was a warm, balmy spring day, and that Welshman's coat glistened in the sun. I knew I had to own one.

Still, realizing a prospective dog owner should never acquire a dog based on appearance alone, I set out to research the breed. Because Welsh Springers are rare in the United States, there is very little literature available about them, so I talked with breeders and other Welsh Springer owners. Convinced this medium-sized spaniel's temperament, intelligence, and aptitude for training would meet my expectations and that its exercise and grooming requirements were manageable, I set out to find my puppy.

I had to wait nearly a year. But Truepenny's Special Edition, "Chelsea," was well worth the wait. She is all I dreamed of and more. The Welsh's devotion to its owner is probably unsurpassed. Chelsea follows me from room to room, sits beneath my desk while I write, and if I'm not careful will march right into the shower after me. I find her loyalty, among her many other fine qualities, quite enchanting.

A few years later, my husband and I decided to buy Chelsea a companion. When you fall in love with a breed, it's only natural to take an interest in its "canine cousins." We wanted a dog of about the same size and temperament. My husband was attracted to the deep liver coat of the

The author's spaniels, Chelsea and Smokey.

Field Spaniel. More rare than the Welsh, there is even less written about the Field. So again, I contacted breeders to learn about this spaniel's personality. Soon certain we would be equally happy with a Field, we bought Bitterblue's Bolero, "Smokey." I believe he was the only puppy of his breed available on the East Coast at the time.

That first year was a doozie. Smokey had incredible energy and knew no boundaries. He knocked Chelsea over without hesitation, stole her food and toys, and generally made her miserable. But in time, with maturity and training, he grew into a gentle and loyal dog endearing himself to the three of us. Smokey loves everyone. He has an incredibly happy-go-lucky attitude that extends itself to all creatures great and small.

Over the years our spaniels have given us the greatest joy. They suit our need for canine companionship perfectly. Our lives would be incomplete without them.

Sporting spaniels are all wonderful dogs, yet each breed has its own unique characteristics. I hope this guide assists you in selecting the one that is just right for you. If you have already purchased a puppy, *The Sporting Spaniel Handbook* should help you better understand the newest member of your family.

Enjoy!

Loren Spiotta-DiMare

Chapter One

Introduction to the Sporting Spaniels

Spaniel History

Spaniels have existed and hunted beside man for centuries. Early references to these charming dogs date as far back as 17 A.D. As with many purebred dogs, an accurate account of their early history is difficult to determine. Because spaniel is a derivative of either the old Spanish for "Hispanola" which means Spain or "espaignol" old French for Spanish dog, it is generally believed that these sporting dogs did indeed originate in Spain.

In his book, *Of Englishe Dogges* (circa 1575), Dr. John Caius, a recognized canine authority, divided the sporting spaniels into two groups: those who primarily hunted on land and those on water. That's not to imply that the land spaniels were incapable of swimming or retrieving waterfowl—which many can and still do. But rather, the larger and more energetic dogs were most often used around lakes and streams retrieving, while the smaller dogs excelled in the field.

Unlike the far-ranging pointers and setters, the spaniel was bred to work close to man, quartering (sweeping) the field in a zigzag pattern and sniffing out quarry within gun range. It was then expected to flush (spring) any birds found and hup (sit) until given a command to fetch and retrieve a downed bird or continue with the hunt.

The Sporting Spaniels

Still prized by many today as hunting dogs, spaniels also reign supreme as family companions. The American Kennel Club (AKC), the primary purebred dog registry in the United States, recognizes 146 dog breeds distinguished by specific traits and abilities and divided into seven categories: Sporting, Hound, Working, Terrier, Toy, Non-Sporting, and Herding. There are nine spaniels recognized in the Sporting Group and described in this book. They are the American Water Spaniel, Clumber Spaniel, Cocker Spaniel, English Cocker Spaniel, English Springer Spaniel, Field Spaniel, Irish Water

An English Springer Spaniel flushes a pheasant.

Spaniel, Sussex Spaniel, and Welsh Springer Spaniel.

The Brittany was once among this group, but because its history was always unique—it pointed instead of flushed game—the spaniel was dropped from its name in the 1980s. It is now considered a pointer.

The American Water Spaniel, a fine flushing and retrieving dog, to this day has not officially been classified as either a spaniel or retriever by the AKC. Devotees fall into either camp, and some believe the breed should receive a dual classification. Regardless, this breed is covered in Chapter Four.

The Irish Water Spaniel is also a bit unique. Bred with an emphasis on retrieving, the Irish Water Spaniel is only eligible to participate in AKC Field Trials and hunting tests for retrievers. It is not allowed to participate in spaniel trials or tests.

Each purebred dog recognized by the AKC is represented by a national parent club, for example the English Cocker Spaniel Club of America. These clubs, which are excellent sources of information, usually publish a breed newsletter or magazine, sponsor dog sporting events, and can provide a list of breeders for prospective spaniel owners. Because officers change periodically, it is best to contact the AKC to request the name of the current club secretary. For more information, see Useful Addresses and Literature, page 139.

The American Spaniel Club (A.S.C.), founded in 1881, sponsors a spectacular Flushing Spaniel Specialty Show in the Northeast each year. Over 700 entrants and equally as many spectators attend the event.

The club also sponsors an annual Cocker Spaniel Show every July in different locations throughout the country. In addition to these shows, the A.S.C. publishes a newsletter, *The A.S.C. Bulletin,* three times a year and an annual report for its members. It also conducts seminars on various spaniel-related topics. For more information contact the AKC, and request the name and address of the current A.S.C. secretary.

Of the 146 breeds recognized by the AKC, the sporting spaniels range from some of the most popular to the most rare. Popularity is determined by the number of registrations in a given year.

Irish Water Spaniels are only eligible to compete in Field Trials and Hunting Tests for retrievers.

Much has been published about the more popular breeds; however, the lesser known spaniels have been sorely overlooked. All are deserving of recognition. *The Sporting Spaniel Handbook* has been written to introduce the various breeds, offer a comparison, and assist the reader in selecting the best spaniel for their lifestyle.

Whereas information on general care, feeding, and breeding can be found in other books, this guide is designed to describe the personality traits, habits, aptitude for training, and grooming and exercise requirements of each breed. In essence, to give the reader a feel for what it's really like to live with these dogs.

Many spaniel enthusiasts have shared their personal experiences within these pages. New and prospective owners should find their insights interesting and helpful. Long-time devotees will surely learn something novel or at the very least smile at a story that rings true.

Registration Statistics for 1998

Breed	Rank	Registrations
Cocker Spaniel	13	34,632
English Springer Spaniel	27	11,578
English Cocker Spaniel	77	1,174
Clumber Spaniel	115	254
American Water Spaniel	117	223
Welsh Springer Spaniel	118	217
Field Spaniel	127	153
Irish Water Spaniel	131	115
Sussex Spaniel	136	92

Of the breeds described in this book, a few are still bred today to work in the field or fill the role of show dog (pet dogs come from show-bred lines). This division is so keen in the English Springer, for example, that the two types look like entirely different breeds. Certainly, many show-bred dogs can hunt, and many do with great enthusiasm. However, for those who like the breeds with two lines and whose primary interest in obtaining a spaniel is to own a highly motivated gun dog, field-bred dogs are probably the way to go. A list of field-bred dog breeders can be obtained from Sandy Henriques, Associate Publisher of *Spaniels in the Field,* a quarterly magazine. *Spaniels in the Field* and *Gun Dog,* a bimonthly magazine, are excellent publications for hunting enthusiasts. Both include field-bred breeder advertisements. See Useful Addresses and Literature, page 139, for further information.

Although I have mentioned the division between show and field-bred dogs where appropriate, the focus of this guide is on show/pet dogs. With the exception of the water spaniels, all of the dogs included in this book generally have their tails docked—bobbed to a shorter length soon after birth. Some European imports have natural full-length tails.

Two English Springers on the go.

Breed Comparison Charts

American Water Spaniel

Height:	15–18 inches (39–47 cm)
Weight:	
dogs:	38–45 pounds (17.1–20.2 kg)
bitches:	25–40 pounds (11.2–18 kg)
Coat:	can range from marcel (uniform waves) to closely curled.
Coat colors:	solid liver, brown, or dark chocolate. A little white on toes and chest permissible.
Feathering:	n/a
Activity level:	medium
Amount of barking:	low (higher for females)
Need for affection:	medium
Dominance over owner:	medium to high
Aptitude for training:	high
Ease of housebreaking:	high
Exercise required:	medium
Shedding:	medium
Trimming/grooming needed:	low

Clumber Spaniel

Height:
    dogs: 19–20 inches (50–51 cm)
    bitches: 17–19 inches (44–50 cm)
Weight:
    dogs: 70–85 pounds (31.5–38.2 kg)
    bitches: 55–70 pounds (24.7–31.5 kg)
Coat colors: primarily white with lemon or orange markings. Freckles on the muzzle and forelegs are common.

Feathering: moderate
Activity level: medium
Amount of barking: low
Need for affection: high
Dominance over owner: low to medium
Aptitude for training: medium
Ease of housebreaking: high
Exercise required: medium
Shedding: high
Trimming/grooming needed: medium

Breed Comparison Charts (continued)

Cocker Spaniel

Height:

dogs:	15 inches (39 cm)
bitches:	14 inches (36 cm)
Weight:	not specified in the standard.
Coat colors:	three varieties

Black: solid black or black with tan points.
ASCOB: (Any Solid Color Other than Black)
Any solid color other than black, ranging
from lightest cream to darkest red, including
brown and brown with tan points.
Parti-Color: Two or more solid, well-broken
colors, one of which must be white; black
and white, red and white, brown and white,
and roans, including those with tan points.

Feathering:	heavy
Activity level:	medium
Amount of barking:	low to medium
Need for affection:	high
Dominance over owner:	low
Aptitude for training:	high
Ease of housebreaking:	medium to high
Exercise required:	medium
Shedding:	medium
Trimming/grooming needed:	high

Breed Comparison Charts (continued)

English Cocker Spaniel

Height:	
dogs:	16–17 inches (42–44 cm)
bitches:	15–16 inches (39–42 cm)
Weight:	
dogs:	28–34 pounds (12.6–15.3 kg)
bitches:	26–32 pounds (11.7–14.4 kg)
Coat colors:	blue roan, black, red, black and white, liver and white, black/white and tan, liver/white and tan, blue roan and tan, liver roan, liver roan and tan, orange and white, orange roan, black and tan, solid liver, and liver and tan.
Feathering:	moderate to heavy
Activity level:	medium to high
Amount of barking:	medium
Need for affection:	high
Dominance over owner:	low
Aptitude for training:	medium
Ease of housebreaking:	medium
Exercise required:	medium
Shedding:	medium
Trimming/grooming needed:	medium

Breed Comparison Charts (continued)

English Springer Spaniel

Height:
dogs:	20 inches (52 cm)
bitches:	19 inches (50 cm)

Weight:
dogs:	50 pounds (22.5 kg)
bitches:	40 pounds (18 kg)

Coat colors:	black and white, liver and white, blue or liver roan, and tricolor
Feathering:	moderate to heavy
Activity level:	high
Amount of barking:	low to medium
Need for affection:	high
Dominance over owner:	low
Aptitude for training:	high
Ease of housebreaking:	high
Exercise required:	medium to high
Shedding:	medium
Trimming/grooming needed:	medium to high

Breed Comparison Charts (continued)

Field Spaniel

Height:	
dogs:	18 inches (47 cm)
bitches:	17 inches (44 cm)
Weight:	40–55 pounds (18–24.7 kg)
Coat colors:	black, liver, golden liver, roan, or any of these with tan points
Feathering:	moderate
Activity level:	medium
Amount of barking:	low
Need for affection:	high
Dominance over owner:	low
Aptitude for training:	medium to high
Ease of housebreaking:	high
Exercise required:	medium
Shedding:	medium
Trimming/grooming needed:	medium

Breed Comparison Charts (continued)

Irish Water Spaniel

Height:
  dogs: 22–24 inches (58–62 cm)
  bitches: 21–23 inches (54–60 cm)
Weight:
  dogs: 55–65 pounds (24.7–29.2 kg)
  bitches: 45–58 pounds (20.2–26.1 kg)
Coat: Topknot on head: long loose curls. Face: short and smooth. Body: tight, crisp ringlets. Legs: curls or waves. Rat tail: two or three inches of curls at root, then short, smooth hair to fine tip.
Coat color: liver
Feathering: n/a
Activity level: high
Amount of barking: low
Need for affection: medium
Dominance over owner: low to medium
Aptitude for training: high
Ease of housebreaking: high
Exercise required: medium to high
Shedding: low
Trimming/grooming needed: medium to high

Breed Comparison Charts (continued)

Sussex Spaniel

Height:	13–15 inches (34–39 cm)
Weight:	35–45 pounds (15.7–20.2 kg)
Coat color:	golden liver
Feathering:	moderate
Activity level:	low to medium
Amount of barking:	low
Need for affection:	medium to high
Dominance over owner:	low
Aptitude for training:	medium
Ease of housebreaking:	medium to high
Exercise required:	medium
Shedding:	medium
Trimming/grooming needed:	low to medium

Breed Comparison Charts (continued)

Welsh Springer Spaniel
Height:
    dogs: 18–19 inches (47–50 cm)
    bitches: 17–18 inches (44–47 cm)
Weight: not specified in the standard
Coat colors: red and white only
Feathering: moderate
Activity level: medium
Amount of barking: medium to high
Need for affection: high
Dominance over owner: low
Aptitude for training: medium to high
Ease of housebreaking: high
Exercise required: medium
Shedding: medium
Trimming/grooming needed: medium

Sports for Spaniels

For many of us, part of the joy in dog ownership is participating in canine sports. The AKC sponsors and sanctions numerous dog shows and performance events throughout the year.

During dog shows, referred to as conformation, dogs are judged on how well they "conform" to a written standard for their breed. A standard, created by a breed's national parent club, for example, The Irish Water Spaniel Club of America, describes the physical and mental attributes the perfect dog of that breed should possess. Complete standards, which are reprinted with permission of each parent club, appear at the close of every chapter.

Performance events test a dog's ability to perform a variety of tasks whether it be executing a set number of exercises in an obedience trial or navigating an agility obstacle course.

Spaniels are athletic dogs that can excel in numerous sports. The following describes each of these activities in greater detail.

Dog Shows

Conformation dog shows are divided into three types: specialty, group, and all-breed. Specialty shows are open to one breed only. Group shows are for an entire group such as Sporting Dogs. And of course, all-breed shows can include every breed recognized by the AKC.

During a conformation show, dogs are competing against their breed standard—an image of what the ideal dog should be—not each other. There are six classes in which to compete, and ultimately the winners of each class compete against each other. Judges evaluate, both visually and by going over the dogs with their hands, the general appearance; head; neck; topline; body, including tail; forequarters; hindquarters; coat color; gait; and temperament. He or she then selects the top four dogs. The first-place picks of each class compete against each

Cocker Spaniels competing in the breed ring.

other. The best of all the first place dogs is the winner and receives points toward its championship. The winner earns from one to five points depending on the number of dogs entered in the breed.

After a dog has accumulated 15 points, including two majors, which are wins of three to five points, it receives its championship of record title and Ch. then appears in front of its registered name. Because dog shows are in part a forum allowing exhibitors to assess future breeding prospects, only intact male and female dogs are allowed to compete.

An English Cocker retrieves on flat in open obedience.

Obedience Trials

Obedience trials create a partnership between handlers and their dogs. Following directions from their owners, obedience dogs must complete a set of exercises that are scored on a basis of 200 points by a judge. Dogs can earn between 20 and 40 points per exercise and must earn at least 170 points and 50% of each exercise to qualify for a "leg" toward their titles. Three legs or qualifying scores complete a title. Conformation has no bearing on this type of competition. Spayed and neutered dogs are eligible to participate.

There are three levels of obedience trial competition with a graduating scale of difficulty. At the Novice level, dogs must master six commands: heel on lead and figure eight, stand for examination, heel free, recall, long sit, and long down. After earning three legs, the Novice dog is awarded a Companion Dog

(CD) title that appears at the end of its registered name.

At the Open level, dogs must complete seven exercises: heel free and figure eight, drop on recall, retrieve on flat, retrieve over the high jump, broad jump, long sit, and long down. After receiving three legs in Open, they are awarded Companion Dog Excellent (CDX) titles.

Dogs working on Utility must complete a signal exercise, two scent-discrimination tests, a directed retrieve, directed jumping, and the moving stand. When they have accumulated three legs at this level, they are given a Utility Dog (UD) title.

Superstars of the obedience world can compete at even higher levels and earn Utility Dog Excellent and Obedience Trial Champion titles. There are also special classes for veterans (dogs over seven years of age), braces (two dogs and one handler), and teams (four people and four dogs competing as a single unit).

Agility Trials

Agility provides another sport that allows dog and owner to work closely together as a team. In fact, the owner runs with the dog directing it through an obstacle course consisting of jumps, weave poles, a seesaw, open and closed tunnels, a dog walk (elevated plank) pause table, and an A-Frame. The direction of the course is determined by the judge at the start of the event.

Not only must the dog execute the obstacles in the proper sequence, the competition is timed. There are also height categories that allow short dogs to compete against other small dogs and long-legged breeds against other tall dogs. Dogs receive faults for such errors as refusing, going over the wrong obstacle, and knocking down a jump. Running the course beyond the time allowed also results in a penalty. The dog with the least amount of faults and the fastest time wins.

There are four levels of agility competition. At each level, the course becomes more demanding. A dog must successfully complete three courses under two different judges to earn a title at that level. Titles that can be achieved are: Novice Agility (NA), Open Agility (OA), Agility Excellent (AX), and Master Agility (MX). To earn the MX a dog must pass ten times at the Agility Excellent level

In AKC events, only purebreds who are at least one year old are eligible to compete. However, trials are held by other organizations, such as the United States Dog Agility Association, that allow mixbreeds to participate.

In order to do well in agility, dogs must not only be athletic, they need to reliably respond to obedience commands. Courses are run off-leash, and there are numerous distractions, usually including an enthusiastic group of spectators.

Tracking

Tracking, as its name implies, tests a dog's ability to follow, "track," a human scent. There are three levels of difficulty in this sport. In order to receive a title, a dog need only successfully complete one track in each level. However, it must pass a practice or certification track under one judge before entering a tracking test.

To earn a Tracking Dog (TD) title, a dog must negotiate a 440- to 500-yard (39.6–45-m) track, including prescribed turns, which was laid

Cocker Spaniels love the excitement of agility. This buff maneuvers the weave poles.

down by tracklayers thirty minutes to two hours beforehand, and indicate a glove at the end of the track.

To receive a Tracking Dog Excellent (TDX) title, a 800- to 1,000-yard (72–90-m) track is laid down that has physical and scent obstacles, as well as four articles that can include wallets, glasses, and gloves in addition to more turns. The dog must successfully follow the track, which is three to five hours old.

The Variable Surface Tracking (VST) title is earned when a dog follows a scent through streets and around buildings or other trails with and without areas of vegetation.

If a dog is awarded all three titles, it becomes a Champion Tracker.

A Field Spaniel tracking.

Field Trials

Field trials showcase the work spaniels were bred for: hunting. They are highly competitive, usually dominated by field-bred English Springers. Cockers and English Cockers are also eligible to participate in their own events. Separate trials are also held for retrievers and pointers.

Courses that emulate hunting situations are created with planted game birds. Dogs are expected to find, flush, and retrieve in an efficient fashion. Intensity, speed, and hard flushes are prized by judges in these competitions. Dogs run a series of courses. In some, they compete in braces—two at a time without interfering with one another. In others, they hunt and are evaluated individually. Dogs are judged on attitude, style, presentation, and control. They are eliminated for such errors as moving out of gun range, never finding the bird, or refusing to retrieve. The top four performing dogs are awarded points toward their championship. There are three trial levels to master. The Amateur Field Champion (AFC) level is open to owners handling their own dogs. They cannot be professional trainers or field dog trial handlers. In addition to winning on the field to earn the AFC, the dog must retrieve from water. The Field Champion (FC) level is open to both amateurs and professionals. To earn the FC the dog must also retrieve from water.

The National Amateur Field Champion and National Field Champion events are the Super Bowls of the field trialing world. Each is held annually, which gives competitors only one chance a year to become a national champion.

Hunting Tests

Unlike field trials where dogs are judged against one another, in a hunting test they are evaluated by an expected standard of performance. Seven areas of evaluation include: steady on line, quartering efficiently, finding and flushing birds, marking downed birds, retrieving on land, retrieving from water, and a display of gun shyness. They are scored from one to ten by two judges. Dogs must earn at least a seven to pass each area. Though these tests are less competitive than field trials, they are an exciting challenge for both dog and handler.

Similar to other AKC sporting events there are various levels of participation with graduating degrees of difficulty. More control and precision is expected at each level. For example, a dog must retrieve from water at the junior level, and it must bring the bird within close proximity to its owner but not

A Welsh Springer retrieves a dummy in training.

necessarily to hand. At the senior level, the dog is expected to deliver to hand.

To earn a Junior Hunter (JH) title, dogs need to qualify in four tests at this level. The Senior Hunter (SH) title is awarded after qualifying in five senior tests. However, if a dog already has a JH, it only needs to pass four times. To become a Master Hunter (MH), a dog needs to compete and qualify in six senior-level tests. If it already has an SH, it only needs to qualify in five senior-level tests.

Working Certificate Tests

In addition to trials and hunting tests sponsored by the AKC, each spaniel breed club conducts its own Working Certificate Test programs. These tests, conducted on land and water, while not sanctioned by the AKC, offer pet owners, exhibitors, and others the opportunity to participate in hunting activities. It also allows dogs from show-bred lines to flaunt their field abilities.

Any flushing spaniel is eligible to run in a test sponsored by another spaniel breed club. However, the sponsoring club must solicit approval from those parent clubs whose members plan to participate. If a dog earns a title, its parent club issues the certificate.

Flyball

Flyball is a relay race for dogs. The course consists of four hurdles with a spring-loaded ball box at the end. There are four canine competitors on a team who run the course individually. After a dog jumps the last hurdle it must step on the box, which causes a tennis ball to pop out. The dog catches the ball, turns around, and jumps over the hurdles again. When it passes the start line the next competitor goes. The first team to have all four dogs run without any mistakes and the best time wins.

The height of the hurdles depends on the size of the dogs on the team. They are set four inches (10.5 cm) below the shoulder height of the shortest dog. Individual dogs earn points toward titles based on the team's time. If the course is run in less than 32 seconds, one point is earned. Less than 28 seconds, five points are earned, and less than 24 seconds, 25 points are earned.

There are many flyball titles to achieve based on an accumulation of points: Flyball Dog (FD), Flyball Dog Excellent (FDX), Flyball Dog Champion (FDCh), Flyball Master

An English Cocker competing in a scent hurdle race—a sport similar to flyball.

(FM), Flyball Master Excellent (FMX), Flyball Master Champion (FMCh), the ONYX AWARD, and Flyball Grand Champion.

Flyball is not a recognized AKC sport. It is sponsored by the North American Flyball Association. Fast, ball-crazy dogs, which many spaniels are, will love flyball.

Chapter Two

Preventive Health Care

Selecting a Veterinarian

Selecting a competent and caring veterinarian is an integral step in achieving optimal wellness for your spaniel. I have the utmost respect for the veterinary profession. After all, a vet acts as your dog's pediatrician during puppyhood, primary care physician and dentist throughout its adult life, and surgeon when the need arises. Obviously, animal patients can't communicate "where it hurts" or why they don't feel well. So veterinarians must be exceptional diagnosticians as well as clinicians.

It's best to choose a vet before actually acquiring your new dog or puppy. Ask pet-owning friends for recommendations. Then schedule an interview with one or two who seem promising.

While it's essential to find a veterinarian who will provide sound medical advice and care, personal rapport is also important. Remember you will have a relationship with this person for the next decade or more.

Most pet owners are extremely attached to their canine compan-ions. So a good vet will patiently listen to and address their clients' questions and concerns. He or she should explain medical conditions in layman's terms as well as the purpose of prescribed medications and procedures.

During the initial meeting ask:
• how much time is usually allotted for an exam,
• if an attendant is on duty all evening should your pet require surgery and need to stay overnight,
• if the hospital provides emergency care after hours or do they refer to an emergency clinic,
• when the vet returns phone calls.

I'm fortunate to have found a wonderful veterinarian who takes my calls immediately when possible or within an hour or two. Some vets return calls late in the evening. It's always best to know beforehand.

Also request a tour of the facilities. It should be clean and appear well managed. At this time, you might inquire about fees for routine exams, vaccinations, spay/neuter operations, teeth cleaning, parasite tests, and medications.

Once you have acquired your pup or adult spaniel, schedule an appointment with the vet you have selected within the first week. Together you will embark on a plan to give your new family member the best possible care.

Veterinary medicine has become very sophisticated. Many of the diagnostic tools and treatments used for humans are also available for pets. Of course, higher costs are often associated with better technology. Fortunately, health insurance covering preventive and emergency care can now be obtained for animals in many states. Acquiring insurance early on is cost effective and can ease the burden of making a medical decision based on financial factors later on. For more information, see Useful Addresses and Literature, page 139.

Dental Care

Once considered frivolous, tooth brushing has become an important part of maintaining canine health. Due to the shape and slant of their teeth, dogs rarely develop cavities. However, various forms of gum disease are common. The modern canine diet does not provide the necessary tearing and chewing action that keeps wild animals' teeth healthy. Soft foods, in particular, stick to tooth crevices and promote bacterial growth. Furthermore, poor oral hygiene can lead to improper digestion, tonsillitis, gastrointestinal problems, and even cardiovascular disease.

Veterinarians must be equally patient with pets and their owners.

While hard foods and biscuits and safe dog chew toys may help ward off trouble, routine preventative care, brushing a pet's teeth at least three times a week, is best.

Getting a dog to accept having its teeth brushed is a gradual process. Begin by letting it become accustomed to having you run your finger along its gums. After a week or two try using a gauze pad or wash cloth moistened with water. Lift your dog's lips and slowly massage the upper teeth. Several days later add a dog toothpaste. These come in tasty flavors like poultry and are often easily accepted. Do not use human toothpaste as it can cause digestive upset.

When your dog appears ready, replace the gauze pad or washcloth with a specially designed dog toothbrush or a child's toothbrush. Gently

Many spaniels are prone to ear infections.

brush the outside of the upper teeth and gums in a circular motion for about 30 to 60 seconds. Then open your pet's mouth and brush the lower teeth and whatever other areas you can reach.

Many pets learn to accept having teeth brushed and some never do. In either case, an annual routine cleaning by a veterinarian may be necessary.

Ear Care

Because of their long pendulous ear flaps that block proper air circulation to the inner ear, many spaniel breeds are prone to painful ear infections. Continual preventive measures are often required.

Keeping the inside ear flap trimmed and free of excess hair is helpful. Be sure to gently insert a cotton ball in the ear before using elec-tric clippers to prevent hair from falling into the canal. You may also trim the upper portion of the outer ear flap. Some spaniel owners tie ears back with a hair clip or hair band periodically to promote air circulation.

Ears should be cleaned twice a week with a cotton ball and appropriate cleanser available through veterinarians and pet shops. If despite these precautions you notice an odor or accumulated debris in the ear or your dog shakes its head frequently and scratches at its ears, make an appointment with the vet. Ear problems are most frequently attributed to an overgrowth of yeast, bacteria, or the presence of mites. Only a veterinarian can properly diagnose the problem and prescribe the appropriate medication.

Owners of the longer-eared spaniels find ears usually fall into food bowls and create quite a mess. Wearing a snood (tubelike hat) or tying the ears up with a hair band solves the problem nicely. Snoods are often available through dog supply catalogs.

Parasite Control

Dogs are often plagued by external and internal parasites. Fleas, ticks, and worms, particularly heartworms, are of greatest concern.

Fleas

Fleas can be the bane of the dog's, and its owner's, existence. These tiny parasites bite and suck blood from their canine hosts causing itching and discomfort. Capable jumpers, they're not adverse to landing on people and taking a meal. Some dogs are particularly sensitive to flea saliva and develop an intense allergic reaction that is often difficult to treat. As secondary hosts, fleas can also transmit tapeworms.

Although these irritating parasites feed off of dogs, adults actually live and usually lay their eggs elsewhere in the environment. So not only the dog but its bedding, other favorite resting spots, and the yard must be treated. Severe indoor infestations may require the services of a professional exterminator.

Fortunately, there are numerous products to fight fleas on the market, including shampoos, sprays, collar, dips, and internal medications. It's best to discuss options with your vet.

Ticks

Ticks have received a lot of press in recent years as they are known to transmit several serious illnesses. Lyme disease, a debilitating disease that can lead to chronic arthritis, heart problems, and neurological damage, is of particular concern. Once confined to certain pockets of the country, it is rapidly spreading.

There are numerous products available to repel and kill ticks. Still it is best to remove these bloodsucking parasites before they have a chance to latch onto the skin.

Begin by thoroughly examining your spaniel after it has been in a tick-infested area. Deer ticks, one of the primary carriers of Lyme disease, are tiny and particularly difficult to spot. Dog owners have successfully removed various types of ticks with flea combs, adhesive lint brush wheels, and even handheld vacuums if their pets allow it.

If you find a tick embedded in your dog's skin, soak it with a cotton ball dipped in rubbing alcohol. Then grab its head with tweezers or a tick remover (a small spoon-shaped tool with a tiny wedge cut out) and pull gently, taking care not to break it apart. Then drown it in a cup of water with detergent. Complete the procedure by washing the site with an antiseptic.

If despite all efforts to protect your spaniel from ticks and Lyme disease it develops a fever, shows signs of stiffness, begins to limp, and appears lethargic, make an appointment with your veterinarian. When caught in the early stage, the disease can be successfully treated with antibiotics.

This Cocker is wearing a snood.

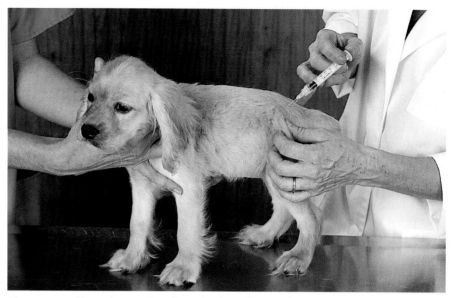

Your puppy will require a series of vaccinations. (Cocker Spaniel)

Internal Parasites

The most common types of internal parasites (roundworms, whipworms, tapeworms, hookworms, and coccidia) live in a dog's intestines. Untreated they can cause lethargy, diarrhea, anemia, and vomiting. Puppies are most susceptible to worm infestation, so when you bring your pup for its first examination by a vet, bring along a stool sample to be tested for parasites. If worms are present, an appropriate medication will be dispensed. Although worms usually affect puppies, it's a good idea to have your dog checked annually throughout its life.

Heartworms are a particularly serious health risk. Carried by mosquitos, these worms, which can grow to a foot long, live in a dog's heart and can eventually cause heart failure.

Treatment of heartworm infestation is difficult and not always successful. Prevention is the best line of defense. A blood test will first be taken to make sure no heartworm larva is present, then a daily or monthly medication will be prescribed.

Vaccinations

Similar to human medicine, immunizations have been developed to protect dogs from infectious canine diseases caused by viruses and bacteria. Administering a vaccine triggers an immune response by building antibodies to fight invading organisms. Because puppies are particularly vulnerable, they are usually vaccinated every two to four weeks between the ages of six weeks and four months.

Although immunizations have done a great deal to control the spread of illnesses in the canine population, they do not offer a guarantee and may prove ineffectual in some individuals.

Traditionally, dogs have been given annual boosters (with the exception of some rabies vaccines that are administered every three years) to continue protection. Recently, many concerned pet owners and members of the veterinary community have begun to question the validity of revaccinating so frequently, the fear being there might be a link between taxing the immune system in this manner and the onslaught of many degenerative diseases. Some vets now recommend, or their clients request, a blood test instead to measure antibody levels in a dog's system. If protective levels are still high, revaccinating may be postponed.

Because the type of immunizations required are in part related to

Spaniel owners should be aware of breed-specific health concerns.

geographic area and the incidence of disease, you should discuss your spaniel's vaccine and booster schedule during the initial visit with your veterinarian.

Note: Concerned with the possible toxicity of traditional parasite control measures, many pet owners are turning to natural remedies. There are a number of holistic pet-care books, magazines, and newsletters now on the market. For more information, see Useful Addresses and Literature, page 139.

Chapter Three

Medical Conditions

The following information describes medical conditions known to occur in spaniels. Breed-specific ailments will be highlighted at the close of each chapter.

Allergies

Like people, some dogs are prone to allergies. In fact, canine skin conditions are most frequently attributed to allergic reactions. Triggers can be almost anything from ingredients in commercial dog foods to pollens and insect bites. Symptoms include rashes, scratching, coughing, tearing, sometimes sneezing, and even vomiting or diarrhea. Obviously, because allergies can be associated with so many catalysts, the specific allergen must be diagnosed so a suitable course of treatment can be prescribed.

Diabetes Mellitus

Diabetes mellitus is caused by an inability of the pancreas to produce sufficient insulin. As a result, sugar in the bloodstream can't be utilized and builds up. The kidneys must work overtime to rid the body of the excess sugar. Affected dogs feel an abnormal need to urinate.

Early signs of diabetes include voracious appetite, large intakes of water, weight loss, and frequent urination. This disease is often successfully controlled with a modified diet and daily insulin shots.

Epilepsy

In general terms, seizure-causing disorders are a result of brief abnormal activity in the brain. The afflicted animal may show signs of anxiety, convulse, drool, urinate, defecate, or fall unconscious. Though seizures are directly related to the brain, the underlying cause may be attributed to problems outside of the nervous system, such as kidney or liver disease.

Some dogs suffer from a condition referred to as inherited or idiopathic epilepsy, which means the cause of the seizure is unknown. Cocker spaniels are among the breeds in which this genetic ailment has been diagnosed.

Depending on the origin of the seizure disorder, treatment will be geared toward eliminating the underlying disease if one is present and controlling the actual seizures with anticonvulsant medications.

The Eyes

Cataracts

A cataract refers to a cloudiness appearing over the lens of the eye. It can be just a small spot or grow large enough to cause blindness. Depending on severity, a dog may be able to adjust to the impairment. For more serious cases, surgery is available. Cataracts are inherited in some breeds.

Cherry Eye

A red gland protruding from the corner of the eye is known as cherry eye. Sometimes a vet can push the gland back in place and treat the problem with various medications. However, it may reappear weeks or even months later. Surgery is most often required.

Conjunctivitis

Conjunctivitis is an inflammation of the mucous membrane lining the eyelid. Causes can be attributed to dust and dirt, bacterial growth, a viral disease that creates dryness in the eye, or an underlying allergy.

Washing the eyes with warm water or sterile eye drops and keep-ing hair trimmed short around the area may prevent the problem from occurring. If it persists, medical treatment will be necessary.

Dry Eye

Dry eye is caused by decreased or absent tear duct production creating dried-out, painful corneas and possible blindness. Routine eye exams are recommended in breeds known to be susceptible, such as Cockers and Clumbers because the condition can be treated with medications if caught in its early stages.

Ectropion/Entropion

Ectropion is a condition where the eyelid rolls outward. Conversely, entropion causes the lid to roll inward. Both allow irritants to collect. In some cases, daily gentle cleaning with warm water or sterile

Your spaniel will rely on you for proper health care throughout its life. (Welsh Springer)

Irish Water Spaniels are one of the breeds susceptible to hypothyroidism.

eye drops and wiping excess debris beneath the eye will control the problem. Surgery may be required in more serious cases. A veterinary ophthalmologist should be sought out in these circumstances.

Hip Dysplasia

Hip dysplasia is caused by a poor fit between the ball and socket of the hip joints causing varying degrees of lameness. In some dogs, the discomfort is minimal; in others it can be quite severe. Treatments, aimed at relieving pain, may include dietary modifications, medications, or surgery.

Because hip dysplasia can be debilitating, it is of great concern among dog fanciers. Reputable breeders will not breed adult dogs who have been x-rayed and show signs of dysplasia. Although having canine parents with sound hips won't guarantee a pup will never develop problems, it does offer some measure of assurance.

Hypothyroidism

Hypothyroidism develops as a result of insufficient thyroid hormone production. Symptoms vary but include weight gain, lethargy, and hair loss. Some breeds appear to have a predisposition to this condition, which is diagnosed with blood and thyroid stimulation tests. Hypothyroidism can be controlled with synthetic thyroid hormone replacement.

Kidney Disease

Familial renal disease and congenital hypoplasia are two serious diseases that stunt kidney growth. When a dog's relatives have also suffered from this type of kidney retardation it is considered familial or inherited. When there is no family history the disease is deemed congenital.

If only one kidney is affected, the canine patient can survive. Although there are some supportive measures for dogs with two affected kidneys, the prognosis is very poor. Most succumb at a very early age.

English Cockers may develop lipfold pyoderma.

Lipfold Pyoderma

Lipfold pyoderma refers to infections of the lipfold. Rarely serious, it can be uncomfortable as well as a nuisance. Although a veterinarian can prescribe an appropriate medication or wash, the best treatment is prevention. Hair along the lipfold should be trimmed short at all times.

Seborrhea

An abnormal skin condition, there are two types of seborrhea, oily and dry. With the former, an overproduction of skin oil causes scales and skin patches on the coat and creates an unusual odor. Although there is no actual cure, this kind of seborrhea can be controlled with special shampoos. Medications are also available to relieve discomfort.

Dry seborrhea is characterized by scaly skin resembling dandruff. This type is usually secondary to allergies and bacterial infections. A thorough exam should be performed to diagnose the underlying cause of the problem.

The American Veterinary Medical Association has a comprehensive website for canine health information. Contact: www.avma.org

Chapter Four

The American Water Spaniel

History

In the soft glare of the morning sun, a canoe glides silently along the lake hugging the shore line. Aboard, a hunter and his curly brown spaniel watch and wait. The dog is intent—his body coiled for action. Moments later a shot rings out. The dog lunges into the icy water toward the downed duck. Despite the cold he swims with heart and determination, just as his ancestors before him.

Born and bred to hunt, little has changed for American Water Spaniels. They are one of only five

The American Water Spaniel swims with heart and determination.

breeds exclusively developed in the United States. Their origins begin in the upper Midwest, particularly the Wolf and Fox River Valley regions of Wisconsin. During the early to mid-1800s, market hunters, men struggling to survive in a harsh environment by selling what they were able to hunt or trap, needed practical dogs—those able to flush and retrieve all types of game on land and in the water. They had to be small and compact, easy to carry in and out of a skiff (light rowboat), and obviously able to withstand cold water temperatures. At home, these versatile canine hunters would also have to serve as companions and protectors.

Origin of the Breed

To create such a dog, the English Water Spaniel, an ancient and now extinct breed, was most likely crossed with the Irish Water Spaniel, the Curly-Coated Retriever, and possibly the Field or Sussex Spaniel. In those early years, the resulting breed was known as the Brown Water Spaniel, the American Brown Water Spaniel, or simply Browns,

Indian Browns, American Browns, or Brownies. Medium-sized dogs of about forty pounds (18 kg), their thick curly brown coats protected them from harsh weather, cold water, and briars. They were used to hunt prairie chicken, ruffed grouse, fur-bearing animals, and of course waterfowl.

Some hunters of the time carried "tag teams" of these little brown spaniels to guarantee a full day of hunting. When one group of dogs tired, another team would be sent out to complete the job. These versatile canine hunters were also used as "jump-shooting retrievers." Dog and master would crawl together through the marsh and surprise unsuspecting ducks. Startled, they would take to the air and become easy targets at such close range.

In ensuing years, this functional, well-rounded breed started to lose prominence. First the marshes and subsequently the duck population began to dwindle. Second, a shift began to take place in society as hunting became a sport as opposed to a means of survival. The age of specialization had arrived. Setters, pointers, and flushing spaniels worked upland game, while large retrievers were used on waterfowl. The little brown spaniel may well have become extinct if not for the efforts of one man, Dr. Fred J. Pfeiffer of New London, Wisconsin.

An avid hunter since boyhood, Dr. Pfeiffer had a great fondness for his all-around curly brown gun dog. He established Wolf River Kennels,

A versatile hunter, the American Water Spaniel was developed in the United States.

which held as many as 132 dogs, to perpetuate the breed. This devoted American Water Spaniel enthusiast touted the virtues of his spaniels at every opportunity. Due to his efforts a breed club was established as well as a written standard. The American Water Spaniel was recognized by the United Kennel Club (UKC—second-largest all-breed purebred dog registry) in 1920, the *Field Dog Stud Book* (bird dog registry) in 1938, and the American Kennel Club in 1940. It is fitting that "Curly Pfeiffer," Dr. Pfeiffer's own dog, was the first American Water Spaniel registered with the UKC.

The Breed Today

In the field today, water spaniels are less exuberant and flashy than

English Springers. However, what they lack in panache they make up for in talent. On land they're said to be as skilled as Labradors or Golden Retrievers. Tough and determined, they tend to stay close to the gun and are easy for the sportsman to follow on foot. They're good all-around hunting dogs with a great nose and a nice natural hunting pattern. They will find whatever is shot, no matter how thick the bush or icy the water. And they hunt with lots of enthusiasm and heart. When working on waterfowl, their tails act as rudders, and they can quickly change direction. Although not fast swimmers, they are known for their endurance.

As hunting terrain diminishes in our expanding urban areas, close-working American Water Spaniels make ideal hunting companions. And yet they are one of the rarest dog breeds in the country. It's said there are approximately 3,000 American Water Spaniels in existence at one time. In 1998, only 233 were registered with the AKC. The majority are still found in the Midwest. Of interesting note, the American Water Spaniel has been the state dog of Wisconsin since 1986.

Once referred to as the "poor man's dog" because they were easy to feed and maintain due to their small size, the American Water Spaniel never caught the fancy of the affluent. The well-to-do have the ability to bring recognition to a breed through extensive breeding programs, show campaigns, and other canine sporting events. For the most part, the American Water Spaniel has remained the working man's dog. That's not to say that fanciers of today are not interested in showcasing their dogs' talents in dog sports, but only that their numbers are small.

Classification

In addition to low registration numbers, the American Water Spaniel faces another hurdle: classification. These hardy hunting dogs are neither classified as spaniels or retrievers. Without either distinction the American Water Spaniel may not participate in AKC hunt tests or field trials. Fanciers have debated the issue for years without conclusion. The majority prefer to remain unclassified. At one point, dual classification was suggested but was quickly rejected by the AKC, as it would create havoc with regard to tests and trials. Giving the American Water Spaniel the unfair opportunity to be included in both retriever-only and spaniel-only events would ultimately encourage other sporting breed fanciers to seek dual classification for their dogs. The American Water Spaniel is eligible to run in retriever hunting tests sponsored by the breed's parent club, American Water Spaniel Club, Inc., the Hunt Retriever Club, and the North American Hunting Retriever Association.

Those devoted to having the American Water Spaniel classified as a spaniel formed the American Water

Spaniel Field Association in 1993. Aside from their efforts seeking spaniel classification, the association also sponsors field training sessions, fun hunts, and training seminars.

Breed Description

Because of a lack of passing fads and fashion, American Water Spaniels remain virtually unchanged from their ancestors. Medium-sized, liver-colored dogs, American Water Spaniels stand 15 to 18 inches (39–42 cm) at the shoulder and weigh between 25 and 45 pounds (11.2–20.2 kg). Their distinctive waterproof coats can be tightly curled or fall in waves known as a "marcel pattern." Their tails, moderately long and left undocked, are slightly feathered.

These unique-looking spaniels are sometimes confused with Irish Water Spaniels—much larger, brown, curly-coated dogs. The Irish stands between 21 and 24 inches (54–62 cm) and weighs between 55 and 65 pounds (24.7–29.2 kg). Also rare, they have curly topknots on their heads and thin, smooth tails. The Irish Water Spaniel is discussed in Chapter Ten.

Never truly catching on in show circles like some of its silky-coated cousins, the American Water Spaniel has not suffered from a division in appearance. Although the English Cocker, for example, has distinct show- and field-bred lines, the typical American Water Spaniel can be a showman and hunter all in one. Note: Some English Cockers from show lines also hunt.

Irish Water Spaniel.

American Water Spaniel.

The American Water Spaniel is sometimes confused with the much larger, brown curly coated Irish Water Spaniel.

Personality

Whereas many spaniel breeds are known for their "soft" sensitive temperaments, American Water Spaniels are hardier souls. They have a mental and physical toughness not usually associated with spaniels. Although affectionate, they tend to be one-family dogs, often bonding to one particular person with whom they share their homes.

Pack Mentality

Dogs generally make wonderful pets because they see their human family unit as a pack—reminiscent of the social groupings formed by wolves, their wild ancestors. To maintain order there must be an Alpha (leader) wolf followed by subordinate members. In human households, one person must become the pack leader in the dog's eyes. Once this relationship is established, dogs feel comfortable in their surroundings because they understand their position. Some breeds and individual dogs accept human leadership more readily than others.

American Water Spaniels are great dogs for some households, but they are not for everyone. They need to live with knowledgeable owners able to establish the Alpha role early on, as most want to be "leader of the pack" and will test their owners' position.

The American Water Spaniel is a primitive breed. For many years they were pack-bred (allowed to live in a group with the dominant male naturally selecting the dominant female as its mate), or the breeder would purposely pair one dominant dog with another to preserve hunting instinct. Little thought was given to appearance or personality, resulting in some dogs with questionable, snappish temperaments. Devoted enthusiasts have since worked diligently and successfully to breed attractive, even-tempered dogs. Still, they require a good amount of interaction with their owners to achieve an enjoyable rapport.

Socialization

American Water Spaniels need lots of early socialization to learn that people are good. If a puppy is left in the kennel or with other dogs in the early stages of development, it will bond to other dogs rather than humans, and it's very difficult, if not impossible, to win it back. Because American Water Spaniels tend to be one-person or one-family dogs, they usually do not work for other people and do not do well being moved

American Water Spaniels require lots of early socialization.

from one family to another. Not surprisingly, because American Water Spaniels have strong personalities, they do well with owners who have the same.

These spaniels are slow to mature and have been known to be stubborn. Yet, the breed does have a sensitive side. Humane, positive methods must be used in training. When treated too roughly, these dogs can become timid or worse, fear biters. Well-adjusted water spaniels are a great joy to their owners. They are intelligent, playful well into their senior years, and eager to please those they care about.

The American Water Spaniel may be initially reserved with unfamiliar children but soon acknowledges well-behaved youngsters as potential playmates and eagerly participates in their games. Some dominant, more aggressive strains of American Water Spaniels still exist. Prospective owners with children should carefully observe the behavior of the dogs in the line they are considering. Generally, the American Water Spaniel has an innate sense of fair play and good humor. To emphasize the point one American Water Spaniel owner reports her female, Katie, is always happy, even when she's in trouble.

Despite their strong hunting heritage, American Water Spaniels can adapt to suburban or even urban life. Their size lends itself to apartment living as long as they are given enough exercise to satisfy their active natures.

The American Water Spaniel has an innate sense of fair play and good humor.

Breed Characteristics

American Water Spaniels offer excellent watchdog protection. They are very alert, quick to give off an alarm, and easy to quiet. Some individuals, however, take the protective barking to extremes—an annoying habit that can be deterred with proper training.

Not surprisingly, American Water Spaniels are cautious about anyone they don't know and protective of their homes and people. They often position themselves between their owners and a stranger until

American Water Spaniels have been known to grin and yodel.

A less endearing behavior is the breed's fondness for "eating anything." They are true "garbage hounds" and have been known to swallow rocks, chunks of cement, pantyhose, children's toys, sticks, and the list goes on. Any breed of dog can ingest a foreign object, but it seems an especially close eye must be kept on American Water Spaniels to keep them out of harm's way.

Training

American Water Spaniels are intelligent dogs. However, they gain their independence early, which means they like to make their own decisions. Yet, at the same time, the breed is slow to mature, which can make training a bit of a challenge.

Because the American Water Spaniel is a one-person dog, that individual should be responsible for training. Because of the strong attachment to its owner, this devoted spaniel is not likely to follow instruction from a professional trainer. Group obedience classes are ideal, providing socialization for the dog as well as structure.

A stoic breed, the water spaniel has an unusually high pain tolerance, which makes harsh training methods ineffectual. Furthermore, these dogs have a strong sense of fair play and simply will not perform for an unfair taskmaster. A firm tone and gentle hand works best. They seem to learn quickly if trained with love and praise. But if the trainer gets angry or

introduced. After proper introductions have taken place, the American Water Spaniel will accept the visitor and act in a friendly manner.

The breed is not always as gregarious with their own kind or other animals. Although most generally get along with dogs, some do not. As for their affinity for other species, they may be less accepting and trustworthy than some of the other spaniels.

In describing the breed's personality, fanciers often refer to their happy natures. Apparently, the American Water Spaniel is also a "talker," and many are known to yodel. Others grin by curling their lips and exposing their teeth. Of course, the bouncy dancing behavior accompanying the grin tells the uninitiated this is indeed a smile not a snarl.

upset, American Water Spaniels sense it quickly and will not respond.

The best training is "play" training. The American Water Spaniel does not take very well to constant, repetitive drills. Training sessions must be kept short and varied. These dogs will balk if pushed too fast.

Prior obedience training is essential for those interested in hunting with their American Water Spaniels. For though the breed has great instincts in the field, these dogs will work for themselves if a bond has not been established between the owner and his canine companion before the team enters the field.

Obviously born for the hunt, American Water Spaniels boast other sporting talents. They've been known to excel in agility, flyball (the first American Water Spaniel earned a FDCh, flyball championship title, from the North American Flyball Association in 1993), and tracking. The latter is certainly not surprising. Although they are easy dogs to show, like some of the other rare breeds it can be difficult to finish a championship. Because they're very athletic and agile, they make great agility dogs, especially due to their fearlessness.

Exercise and Grooming

Because American Water Spaniels are naturally active dogs, they require and deserve a regular routine of exercise. Daily walks, games of fetch, and/or running in safe, confined areas will keep water spaniels in top mental and physical condition. This breed cannot be expected to be a calm and relaxed member of the family if its exercise needs are not met. Lack of physical activity will result in boredom and restlessness, which lead to destructive chewing and other undesirable behaviors. Those who own more than one American Water Spaniel say they enjoy playing together.

Coat

This energetic spaniel has a double coat. The outer, coarser layer repels water and provides protection from briars. The finer, inner coat acts as insulation. This breed has been known to have "doggy odor" due to the oily nature of the coat, which some may find objectionable. On the positive side, American Water Spaniels are relatively easy to keep looking their best. The coat, which is actually about a half inch longer than a Labrador's, should be brushed weekly. Nails should be clipped and ears cleaned at this time as well. As with most spaniels, ear infections can be a problem, so routine attention to preventative ear care is recommended.

Every one to two months, the top of the head, ears, and back legs from the hocks down can be trimmed smooth, and any loose, straggly hairs on the body clipped. Hunters may wish to keep the coat very short to keep burrs from tagging along for the ride.

Breed-Specific Health Concerns

Dealing with burrs seems to be an ongoing struggle for those who hunt with their American Water Spaniels. Although the curly coat protects the dog from the elements, burrs can get buried right down into the undercoat. To combat the problem, some hunters keep their dogs trimmed fairly close to the body, and others add oil to the coat prior to the hunt to simplify the removal process.

To some extent the early practice of pack-breeding American Water Spaniels has had a positive effect on the breed's overall health. When left to their own devices to breed and take care of themselves, a certain amount of natural selection takes place—only the strongest survive.

Today, American Water Spaniels are generally healthy dogs and do not suffer from many of the inherent problems that plague more popular breeds. Some American Water Spaniel owners even boast their canine companions never required veterinary care for illness.

The American Water Spaniel is not a wonderdog, however, with no health concerns. A number of diseases have shown up in the breed. Some are more serious than others. The American Water Spaniel has been known to have cataracts, allergies, and hypothyroidism. Other glandular disorders that can cause baldness have also occurred.

Of greater concern are diabetes, epilepsy, and hip dysplasia. Also, progressional retinal atrophy has been known to occur in the breed.

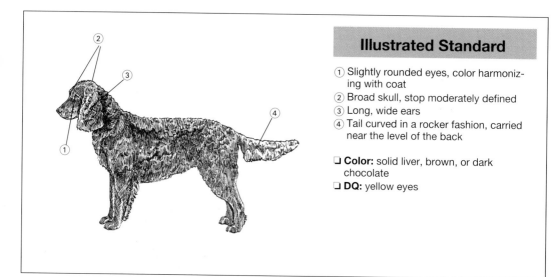

Illustrated Standard

① Slightly rounded eyes, color harmonizing with coat
② Broad skull, stop moderately defined
③ Long, wide ears
④ Tail curved in a rocker fashion, carried near the level of the back

❏ **Color:** solid liver, brown, or dark chocolate
❏ **DQ:** yellow eyes

Official Standard

General Appearance

The American Water Spaniel was developed in the United States as an all-around hunting dog, bred to retrieve from skiff or canoes and work ground with relative ease. The American Water Spaniel is an active muscular dog, medium in size with a marcel to curly coat. Emphasis is placed on proper size and a symmetrical relationship of parts, texture of coat and color.

Size, Proportion, Substance

15 to 18 inches for either sex. Males weighing 30–45 lbs. Females weighing 25–40 lbs. Females tend to be slightly smaller than the males. There is no preference for size within the given range of either sex providing correct proportion, good substance, and balance is maintained. Proportion is slightly longer than tall, not too square or compact. However, exact proportion is not as important as the dog being well-balanced and sound, capable of performing the breed's intended function. Substance, a solidly built and well-muscled dog full of strength and quality. The breed has as much substance and bone as necessary to carry the muscular structure but not so much as to appear clumsy.

Head

The head must be in proportion to the overall dog. Moderate in length. Expression is alert, self-confident, attractive and intelligent. Medium size eyes set well apart, while slightly rounded, should not appear protruding or bulging. Lids tight, not drooping. Eye color can range from a light yellowish brown to brown, hazel, or of dark tone to harmonize with coat. Disqualify yellow eyes. Yellow eyes are a bright color like that of lemon, not to be confused with the light yellowish brown. Ears set slightly above the eye line but not too high on the head, lobular, long, and wide with leather extending to nose. Skull rather broad and full, stop moderately defined, but not too pronounced. Muzzle moderate in length, square with good depth. No inclination to snipiness. The lips are clean and tight without excess skin or flews. Nose dark in color, black, or dark brown. The nose sufficiently wide and with well-developed nostrils to insure good scenting power. Bite either scissor or level.

Neck, Topline, Body

Neck round and of medium length, strong and muscular, free of throatiness, set to carry head with dignity, but arch not accentuated. Topline level or slight, straight slope from withers. Body well-developed, sturdily constructed but not too compactly coupled. Well-developed brisket extending to elbow neither too broad nor too narrow. The ribs well-sprung, but not so well-sprung that they interfere with the movement of the front assembly. The loins strong, but not having a tucked-up look. Tail is moderate in length, curved in a rocker fashion, can be carried either slightly below or above the level of the back. The tail is tapered, lively, and covered with hair with moderate feathering.

Forequarters
Shoulders sloping, clean, and muscular. Legs medium in length, straight, and well-boned but not so short as to handicap for field work or so heavy as to appear clumsy. Pasterns strong with no suggestion of weakness. Toes closely grouped, webbed and well-padded. Size of feet to harmonize with size of dog. Front dewclaws are permissible.

Hindquarters
Well-developed hips and thighs with the whole rear assembly showing strength and drive. The hock joint slightly rounded, should not be small and sharp in contour, moderately angulated. Legs from hock joint to foot pad moderate in length, strong, and straight with good bone structure. Hocks parallel.

Coat
Coat can range from marcel (uniform waves) to closely curled. The amount of waves or curls can vary from one area to another on the dog. It is important to have undercoat to provide sufficient density to be of protection against weather, water, or punishing cover, yet not too coarse or too soft. The throat, neck and rear of the dog well-covered with hair. The ear well-covered with hair on both sides with ear canal evident upon inspection. Forehead covered with short smooth hair and without topknot. Tail covered with hair to tip with moderate feathering. Legs have moderate feathering with waves or curls to harmonize with coat of dog. Coat may be trimmed to present a well-groomed appearance; the ears may be shaved; but neither is required.

Color
Color either solid liver, brown, or dark chocolate. A little white on toes and chest permissible.

Gait
The American Water Spaniel moves with well-balanced reach and drive. Watching a dog move toward one, there should be no signs of elbows being out. Upon viewing the dog from the rear, one should get the impression that the hind legs, which should be well-muscled and not cowhocked, move as nearly parallel as possible, with hocks doing their full share of work and flexing well, thus giving the appearance of power and strength.

Temperament
Demeanor indicates intelligence, eagerness to please, and friendly. Great energy and eagerness for the hunt yet controllable in the field.

Disqualification
Yellow eyes.

Approved March 13, 1990
Effective May 1, 1990
© 1998 by the American Kennel Club.
Courtesy of the American Water
Spaniel Club, Inc.

Chapter Five
The Clumber Spaniel

History

Two massive, silky white spaniels with a touch of lemon about their ears lounge together on the couch. His front paw drapes over the edge as she gently clutches her favorite toy. They are the picture of regal canine decorum as befits the Clumber Spaniel, a breed once owned by British royalty.

The mailman arrives. She awakens. So deep in sleep, he does not. Her quick movements startle him and together they run to investigate. When she blocks his path, he vaults over her. By the time they reach the door, the mailman is en route to the next house. After a few post-warning barks, the two dogs head back to the couch. Her toy still firmly in her grasp.

Origin of the Breed

The Clumber Spaniel is a dog of curious contradictions. Because of its large size, sedate expression, and pension for napping, people often assume it is the consummate couch potato. Although this characterization may be partly true, the Clumber is first and foremost a sporting dog with a strong hunting drive. Although there are several theories regarding its history, the most widely accepted is that the breed originated in France. Supposedly, the French Duc de Noailles presented his Clumbers to Henry Clinton, the Duke of Newcastle in England, at the beginning of the French Revolution, because he feared the lives of his dogs were in danger. Those who subscribe to this theory are uncertain of the breed's ancestors.

Other canine historians believe the Clumber solely originated in England by crossing the Alpine Spaniel, Basset Hound, or even the Saint Bernard. What is known for certain is the Duke of Newcastle was enamored with the breed and developed a kennel on his land, Clumber Park in Nottingham. Hence the name, Clumber Spaniels. Interestingly, there is a painting of the Duke astride his horse with four of his dogs beside him. They look strikingly like the present day Clumber type.

Clumber Spaniels gained recognition for their excellent ability to flush game in the densest underbrush and

Clumber Spaniels were prized by British royalty.

were prized by British royalty, particularly King Edward VII and later his son, George V, who did much to preserve the Clumber's working ability and conformation.

Both world wars disrupted Clumber breeding programs, but after World War II, some very influential Clumber kennels were established, including Mason, Cuerdon, Showholme, and Anchorfield.

The Clumber's history on this side of the Atlantic is considered to have begun in 1844 when British Lieutenant Venables, stationed in Halifax, Nova Scotia, brought his Clumbers with him. The breed soon became popular in the Ottawa district of Canada. They were eventually introduced to dog fanciers in the United States and became one of the first ten breeds recognized by the AKC in 1884.

The Clumbers of old had exceptional scenting abilities. They were selectively bred to work through very tough, wooded cover. Trained to hunt at a relatively slow pace and track scent trapped within a low canopy of leaves, they were expected to be very thorough. It was not a simple task, because thick cover is difficult to penetrate. Quick, fast-moving dogs could easily get hurt. However, the Clumber's bulk, heavy coat, long and low body coupled with a highly focused attitude made it perfect for these conditions.

The Breed Today

Despite their low registration numbers, 254 in 1998, or perhaps because of them, Clumbers have retained their hunting prowess. Some devotees claim their scenting abilities are second only to Bloodhounds. These spaniels are capable of flushing and retrieving woodcock, grouse, pheasant, quail, dove, and rabbits. Plus, many love to swim, have big webbed feet, and a buoyant coat, so they're very adept at water retrieves.

The Clumber tends to work well within gun range and will even wait for its master to catch up from time to time. This breed is a good choice for the amateur gunner, because it works so close in, and any quarry flushed will be in easy shooting range. They also take to their duties with relatively little formal training and because of the predominantly white coat are easy to spot in the field. If they have a fault, it's that they can tune out or ignore commands simply because they are so focused on the job at hand.

Breed Description

The present day Clumber Spaniel looks very much like its ancestors— long, low, and heavyset. Males stand 19 to 20 inches (50–51 cm) and weigh between 70 and 85 pounds (31.5–38.2 kg). Females are about 17 to 19 inches (44–50 cm) and weigh 55 to 70 pounds (24.7–31.5 kg). The silky white coat may have some lemon or orange markings that usually appear on the head or near the base of the tail. Markings on the body may also be seen but are less desirable. The Clumber has a massive head with a square muzzle. The ears are shorter than many of the other breeds and freckles on the muzzle and front legs are common. This unusually bulky spaniel also carries a thick, docked "sausage" tail.

The present day Clumber Spaniel closely resembles its ancestors—long, low, and heavyset.

Personality

Often referred to as jolly or dogs with "jingle bell" personalities, these spaniels are extremely sweet tempered. They love their families and delight in demonstrating their devotion. They have an admirable whole-rear-end tail wag and the unique ability to greet people by curving their bodies in such a way that their front and back ends come toward you at the same time (referred to as Clumber U-ing or Clumber C-ing), all the while performing a little dance.

These dogs are happiest in the company of their owners, but they're not as clingy as some of the other spaniels. When you first arrive home they want to sit in your lap but after a while will return to a favorite rest-ing spot. One fancier aptly described the relationship by explaining his dogs like him and enjoy his company but are not crazy in their devotion, kind of like an old married couple.

Breed Characteristics

Clumber Spaniels are surprisingly quiet and placid around the house for relatively large dogs. They're friendly and demonstrative without being overbearing. But they do have some very strong personality characteristics. One is an obsessive desire to carry something in their mouths. Whereas other spaniels share this passion, Clumbers have taken it to new heights. They will hang onto their toys throughout the day, hoard playthings belonging to canine housemates, and hold several items at once. Amanda, for example, collects tennis balls. She's able to juggle three balls in her mouth while rolling in a mud puddle or lounging in her kiddie pool.

When someone enters the house, the Clumber is very likely to run off, find, and offer guests the nearest toy. If they're not inclined to accept the gift, the dog will hang onto it until nap time. Then they will doze off with a firm grasp on the toy—almost like a baby with a pacifier.

Clumbers seem to have a trophy mentality about items they carry. It's not enough to have something, you have to know they have it. Recovering from back surgery, Shani discovered a nice, juicy five-pound ham on the counter waiting to be served at

Clumbers are described as having jingle bell personalities.

her owners' holiday party. Shani stood up on her hind legs and using her front paws like hands slid the ham toward her mouth. Although most dogs would quickly devour their find, Shani ran to where the company had gathered to show off her prize. Much to their surprise and dismay I'm sure.

Although the Clumber's incessant need to carry can be charming at times and trying at others, it can also be dangerous. These dogs are not particular and have been known to pick up rocks, pantyhose, shampoo bottles, rubber gloves, and just about anything that is not nailed down. Unfortunately, many have also ingested these foreign objects, requiring emergency surgery. Therefore, owners must be prepared to buy their canine companions numerous indestructible toys preferably larger than the recommended size. They must also Clumber-proof the house by keeping loose items out of the reach of these mischievous spaniels.

Clumbers are bright dogs who often figure things out on their own. They have the curiosity and wonderment of a small child. You can almost see a light turning on in their heads when they make a connection. Clover's owner ran a boarding kennel. One evening the woman brought an ailing kitten into the house. Clover had never seen a cat, but when it meowed at her she ran to her toy box, selected a stuffed cat that meows when squeezed and presented it to her mistress.

The need to carry a plaything starts early.

Clumbers can be extremely focused and single-minded. They will remain in position, fixated for hours waiting for something they want. Gracie has been known to sit, staring at the back door expecting to be let out. She doesn't whine or bark, just sits in a very unobtrusive, determined way until she gets the desired response. She will also stand statuesque beneath the birdcage hoping a piece of bread will fall to the ground. If she waits long enough, it usually does.

Clumbers are also known to be great nappers. Some in fact sleep very deeply. They offer some watchdog protection in that they will bark an alarm if they wake up in time to notice something is amiss. Three burglars broke into a house while the homeowners were in bed on the second floor. They ransacked the home and made their getaway while the resident Clumber on the first floor slept through the whole episode. If Clumbers notice an intruder, they're unlikely to do more than bark.

These spaniels have a mixed reaction to strangers. Although some will bound up to visitors at the door eager to make friends, others prefer to stand back and size you up. They want to meet you but on their own terms and in their own time. Usually within a few minutes, when they realize guests are welcomed by their owners, they'll warm up to them as well.

Clumbers make wonderful playmates for children and particularly enjoy games of fetch and retrieve. They seem to have a great affinity for youngsters, particularly infants, and are protective of their charges. However, because of their strength, children should not be allowed to walk their dogs alone.

Most Clumbers get along well with other dogs and family pets. They particularly like living with their own breed. However, some owners have observed aggression toward cats.

Despite their bulk, Clumber Spaniels are surprisingly limber. Amos demonstrates the point well. When his sibling, Puff, is in his way, he doesn't walk around or knock her down, he simply leaps over her with amazing agility and grace. Though prospective owners may be attracted to a dog that spends much of its time sleeping and is less hyper than some other sporting breeds, they should also keep in mind the Clumber is athletic and active as well.

The Three "S's"

Easygoing, quiet around the house, wonderful with children, Clumber Spaniels sound like perfect companions. But they do have a few traits some dog fanciers will find objectionable. Aptly referred to as the three "S's," Clumbers shed, snore, and slobber. Because of their fine silky coats, these dogs lose hair constantly with more profuse shedding in the spring and fall. They seem to have a pension for getting dirty and delight in rolling in mud puddles and other debris.

These spaniels are also known to snore like chain saws and sling drool when they shake their heads, especially those dogs with very droopy flews (lower lip lines). They're also sloppy water drinkers and have a unique habit of snorting—a soft, piglike grunting sound—when happy. They probably would not be a good choice for those who insist upon having impeccably neat homes.

The Devoted Dog

Perhaps their devotion to man overshadows their maintenance. Clumbers hate being isolated from people and are very forgiving dogs. It's difficult to imagine there being a need for rescue groups within such a rare breed. But indeed there are. Clumbers who have been removed from neglectful homes rehabilitate very easily in a loving environment. When given the attention they deserve, they quickly forgive the sins of the past and truly blossom, bonding closely to their new owners.

Training

Clumber Spaniels are very bright dogs who can be a bit self-serving. Training is easy if the lesson at hand is of interest to them. Oftentimes though they have a "I'll get back to you later" attitude. They absolutely will not respond to harsh training methods, and have been known to plant their paws and refuse to budge if treated unfairly. No amount of cajoling or pulling will have an effect. Some may interpret this stubborn resistance as slow to learn, but in actuality it's an intelligent creature demonstrating a not-so-subtle protest.

In addition to refusing to comply with heavy-handed methods, Clumbers have a short attention span and bore easily. Trainers must do their best to keep sessions lighthearted and fun. Grace, who is an obedience competitor, has been known to lie down and take a nap during training classes. The breed does have a very strong work ethic, however, and becomes completely focused and determined to finish the job. This trait is especially apparent in the field.

Because Clumbers are rare, particularly in certain areas of the country, it can be difficult finding enough competition to finish a championship. And because these spaniels are less flashy than some of the other sporting breeds, getting noticed in the group ring is a struggle. Notably, however, a Clumber Spaniel won Best in Show at the prestigious Westminster Dog Show in 1996.

Clumbers do very well in sports where they can use their scenting abilities. They are absolutely fantastic trackers. Merlin became the first Clumber Spaniel to earn a Variable Surface Tracker title in 1996, which has inspired other Clumber fanciers to become involved in this sport.

Clumbers can successfully compete in hunting tests, though controlling them is sometimes a problem. Owners often find they become selectively deaf to commands when they pick up a scent.

Clumbers are also agile enough to participate in agility. But perhaps the greatest calling of this lovable teddy bear of a dog lies outside of competition. The Clumber makes a wonderful canine therapist. Many programs are available that allow dogs to visit and cheer patients in hospitals and nursing homes. The Clumber's calm demeanor, acceptance of patient infirmities, expressive face, and joy in being hugged are irresistible.

Most Clumbers love to swim and it's a wonderful exercise for them.

Exercise and Grooming

Clumber Spaniels do not demand exercise as many other sporting dogs do. In fact, they're quite content to lounge around the house. The breed has a tendency to put on extra weight, which is detrimental to its back and hips. Therefore, it's very important for Clumber owners to set up and adhere to a routine exercise program. Long walks, games of fetch, and swimming are all good outlets for Clumbers, particularly swimming as it is easier on their joints.

These spaniels would not be appropriate companions for avid joggers or bicyclists who want their dogs to keep pace with them. Clumbers are more of a stop-and-go breed, investigating scents along a trail, taking detours now and then, and even laying down for a brief respite.

Because they are dogs who obviously like to lumber along with their distinctive rolling gait (front foot and opposite back foot moving in unison), owners are often surprised to find Clumbers are also capable of great speed in short spurts. They may well dash off in a flash if a scent catches their interest, ignoring commands to return. For this reason, Clumber breeders often advise new owners to keep their dogs on leash at all times or only allow them their freedom in an enclosed area.

Due to the breed's rapid rate of growth, young dogs up to ten months should not be allowed to play so wildly that they may slide or fall easily, leading to injury.

Coat

Clumbers are one of the easier spaniel breeds to care for. They have a "wash and wear" coat, so to speak, that allows mud to simply fall off when it dries. To avoid matting, the fine, silky coat should be

Clumbers are capable of great speed in short spurts.

combed once or twice a week. Though the ears are relatively short, they are thick, and the breed is prone to ear infections. To increase air circulation and avoid problems, the inner ear flap and area behind the ear can be trimmed with an electric clipper. The hair on the upper outer ear need only be neatened with a thinning sheers (scissor with teeth). A weekly routine cleansing is also recommended.

For an attractive, catlike paw, trim the hair on the paw and between the paw pads with scissors or thinning shears. The hair on the back legs from the hock to the ankle joint should also be trimmed. The tail is left alone except for the flag (excess hair on the tip), which may be clipped off. The fringe under the tail can also be neatened.

Because of the self-cleaning nature of the coat, Clumbers only need to be bathed every three to four months. Unless, of course, they have been rolling in mud puddles.

Show dogs are groomed in much the same manner at more frequent intervals.

Breed-Specific Health Concerns

Because Clumber Spaniels are large-boned, fast-growing dogs, they require premium foods for proper development. Many are prone to food allergies and may need to be fed special nonallergenic diets like lamb and rice. Rapid growth can also cause temporary juvenile lameness in the legs between six and twelve months of age. Bouts of lameness or "growing pains" subside when bone growth is complete.

Clumbers frequently suffer from impacted anal sacs. To prevent problems, it's advisable to have them emptied every few months by a veterinarian. The breed tends to be sensitive to heat; therefore, they should always have access to shade and never left unsupervised in areas where it can become uncomfortably hot.

Remember their strong retrieving instinct can get Clumbers into trouble. Only provide indestructible toys and thoroughly Clumber-proof the house.

Serious Health Concerns

The three most serious health concerns in this unique-looking breed involve the eyes, back, and hips.

Clumbers may suffer from entropion, an inward rolling of the eyelid, and/or ectropion, an outward rolling of the lid. These conditions allow irritants to collect. In some cases, daily gentle cleansing with warm water or sterile eyedrops and wiping the excess debris beneath the eye will control the problem. Surgery may be required in more serious cases. A veterinary ophthalmologist should be sought out in these circumstances, preferably one familiar with the breed.

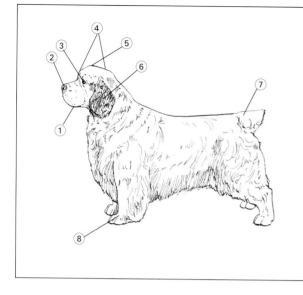

① Well-developed flews
② Nose colored any shade of brown
③ Eyes large, deep-set, diamond shaped; some haw may show
④ Pronounced stop and occiput
⑤ Massive head
⑥ Low-set ears
⑦ Tail docked and carried near horizontal*
⑧ Large feet

❏ **Color:** white dog with lemon or orange markings (the fewer the markings on body, the better)
❏ **DQ:** none

* Clumbers in some European countries may have undocked tails.

Clumbers are also susceptible to dry eye. Routine eye exams are recommended, particularly because this condition can be treated with medication if caught in its early stages.

Because of their long, low backs and weight, Clumbers are prone to herniated discs of the back and neck. These conditions can come on gradually, as a result of injury, or without warning. Depending on severity, close confinement, drugs to reduce swelling, or surgery may be required. Unfortunately, in some cases euthanasia is necessary. To help avoid problems, Clumber owners should keep roughhousing to a minimum and avoid jerking on their dogs' necks. A regular though not vigorous exercise routine to avoid excess weight gain is also very important.

As a breed with a small gene pool, Clumbers are considered clinically hip dysplastic, which means most individuals have some form of hip dysplasia. However, because of their massive, muscular rears that support hip joints, these spaniels don't suffer the same debilitating effects as other breeds with this condition.

Clumbers often have difficulty conceiving and giving birth. Caesarian sections are not uncommon. Some are also sensitive to anesthesia.

Official Standard

General Appearance

The Clumber is a long, low, heavy dog. His heavy brow, deep chest, straight forelegs, powerful hindquarters, massive bone, and good feet all give him the power and endurance to move through dense underbrush in pursuit of game. His white coat enables him to be seen by the hunter as he works within gun range. His stature is dignified, his expression pensive, but at the same time, he shows great enthusiasm for work and play.

Size, Proportion, Substance

Males are about 19 to 20 inches at the withers, bitches are about 17 to 19 inches at the withers. Males weigh between 70 and 85 pounds, bitches between 55 and 70 pounds. The Clumber possesses massive bone and is rectangular in shape. Length to height is approximately 11 to 9 measured from the withers to the base of the tail and from the floor to the withers.

Head

The head is massive. The eyes are dark amber in color, large, soft in expression, deep set in either a diamond shaped rim or a rim with a "V" on the bottom and a curve on the top. Some haw may show. Prominent or round shaped eyes are to be penalized. Excessive tearing, evidence of entropion or ectropion are to be penalized. Ears are broad on top, set low, and attached to the skull about eye level. They are triangular in shape with a rounded lower edge. They are slightly feathered with straight hair, and ear leather is thick. The top skull is flat with a pronounced occiput. A slight furrow runs between the eyes and up through the center of the skull. Marked stop, heavy brow. The muzzle is broad and deep to facilitate retrieving many species of game. The nose is large, square, and colored shades of brown, which includes beige, rose, and cherry. The flews of the upper jaw are strongly developed and overlap the lower jaw to give a square look when viewed from the side. A scissors bite is preferred.

Neck, Topline, Body

The Clumber should have a long neck, with some slackness of throat or presence of dewlap not to be faulted. The neck is strong and muscular and fits into well laid back shoulders. The back is straight, firm, long, and level. The chest is both deep and wide. The brisket is deep. The ribs are well sprung. The loin is only slightly arched. The tail should be docked in keeping with the overall proportion of the adult dog. The tail is set on just below the line of the back and is normally carried parallel to the ground.

Forequarters

The Clumber shoulder is well laid back. The humerus or upper arm is of sufficient length to place the elbow under the highest point of the shoulder. The forelegs are short, straight, heavy in bone with elbows held close to the body. Pasterns are strong and only slightly sloped. The feet are large, compact, and have thick pads which act as shock absorbers. Dewclaws may be removed. The hair may be trimmed for neatness and utility in the field.

Hindquarters

The thighs are heavily muscled, and when viewed from behind, the rear is round and broad. The stifle shows good functional angulation, and hock to heel is short and perpendicular to the ground. Lack of angulation is objectionable. The feet on the rear legs are neither as large, nor as round as on the forelegs, but are compact, have thick pads, and are of substantial size.

Coat

The body coat is dense, straight, flat, and is of good weather resistant texture; it is soft to the touch, not harsh. Ears are slightly feathered with straight hair. Feathering on the legs and belly is moderate. The Clumber has a good neck frill and on no condition should his throat be shaved. The feet may be trimmed to show the natural outline, as well as the rear legs up to the point of hock. Tail feathering may be tidied. Trimming of whiskers is optional. No other trimming or shaving is to be condoned.

Color and Markings

The Clumber is primarily a white dog with lemon or orange markings. Marking around one eye, both eyes, or white face are of equal value.

Freckles on the muzzle and forelegs are common. The fewer markings on the body, the better, although a spot near the root of the tail is common.

Gait

The Clumber moves easily and freely with good reach in front and strong drive from behind, neither crossing over nor elbowing out. The hocks drive in a straight line without rocking or twisting. Because of his wide body and short legs, he tends to roll slightly. The proper Clumber roll occurs when the dog with correct proportion reaches forward with rear legs toward the center line of travel and rotates the hip downward while the back remains level and straight. The gait is comfortable and can be maintained at a steady trot for a day of work in the fields without exhaustion.

Temperament

The Clumber is a loyal and affectionate dog; sometimes reserved with strangers, but never hostile or timid.

Approved October 10, 1989
Effective November 30, 1989
© 1999 by the American Kennel Club.
Courtesy of the Clumber Spaniel Club
of America

Chapter Six
The Cocker Spaniel

History

He sits quietly in the young girl's lap posing politely for the camera. His silky golden ears cascade over his shoulders. The light catches the twinkle in his eyes—dark, brown, loving. He pants just a little and appears to be smiling. The girl hugs him closer as the two are photographed for an advertisement. With his cuddly looks and sweet expression there is no doubt the Cocker's charm will contribute to a winning ad campaign. And it's not surprising, the American public has long had a love affair with the Cocker Spaniel. In 1938, the breed was the most popular dog in the country—a position it held for fourteen years. In the 1950s, interest waned but resurged in the 1980s. Clinging to number one in registrations until 1991, the Cocker continues to rank in the AKC's top fifteen breeds to this day.

Origin of the Breed

Though originally bred to hunt, an instinct many still retain, the Cocker Spaniel reigns as family pet and lapdog supreme. Unfortunately,

unprecedented popularity has taken a toll on the breed's health and temperament. But first a look at its past.

In the early 1800s, Springers and Cockers often appeared in the same litter. Dogs over 25 pounds (11.2 kg), usually liver and white in color, were trained to spring upland game. Their smaller brethren, those under 25 pounds (11.2 kg) and found in a variety of colors, were taught to hunt woodcock, a small, agile bird that lives in marshy areas thick with dense cover. These dogs were aptly referred to as woodcockers or cocking spaniels. In 1902, the Kennel Club (the AKC equivalent in England) separated the breeds and recognized the large dogs as English Springer Spaniels and the smaller simply as Cocker Spaniels.

Within this Springer/Cocker separation, two types of Cockers began to emerge. Both can trace their origins to Obo, a black spaniel whelped in 1879. Obo sired many progeny who were relatively long and low to the ground but hardy enough to hunt. One of his sons, Obo II, owned by F.F. Pitcher, a New England Breeder, is considered the

The ever popular Cocker Spaniel.

father of the (American) Cocker Spaniel.

Cocker history then becomes a little complicated. British breeders felt the long, low dogs were not as well-suited for hunting as they could be. So they began to develop a leggier spaniel with a longer, stronger neck and more refined head. This type, which eventually became known as the English Cocker Spaniel, is discussed in Chapter Seven. The American version remained truer to the original.

During the early 1900s both types of Cockers were imported and exported between British and American breeders. To further confuse mat-

ters, the dogs were often interbred. Eventually in 1921, Red Brucie was bred by Herman Mellenthin in the United States. This attractive Cocker and his offspring set the standard for the proper American type. Over the years, breeders perfected the compact body, rounded head, and heavily feathered coat. Although we refer to these dogs as Cocker Spaniels, to the rest of the world they are known as American Cocker Spaniels.

Meanwhile, in 1881 a group of fanciers had created the American Cocker Spaniel Club and later changed its name to the American Spaniel Club. It remains the parent club for the Cocker Spaniel today.

The Breed Today

Though small, the Cocker was expected to hunt through thick rugged terrain, find game, and flush it into the air. Cockers still retain that bold confidence. They have a large dog spirit wrapped in a compact canine package.

The Hunting Instinct

Some hunting enthusiasts will claim show-bred Cockers have all but lost their hunting prowess, but others will counter that these hardy little dogs have rarely been given the opportunity to prove their abilities. In reality, Cockers can be quite "birdie" (possessing a strong, enthusiastic bird hunting instinct). For some the only chance to use their talents may be in standing vigil over the backyard bird feeder. But there are those successfully working in the field.

Cockers with a strong hunting drive are quite adept at pursuing quail, chukar, dove, and, of course, woodcock. Although they stand less than 16 inches (42 cm) high, these spaniels have an inflated self-image and seem to think they're much larger than they are. Some have successfully retrieved pheasant but are at a disadvantage in retrieving these bigger birds due to their size.

Cockers love to swim and have the will to retrieve waterfowl. Ducks are OK in warm weather conditions but despite its "can do" attitude, they should not be sent out to retrieve geese.

These energetic spaniels hunt at a good pace though closer in than the fast-moving Springer and tend to have a softer flush—approaching their quarry at a slower more cautious pace. They excel at routing out game hidden in tight, deep cover, and are fearless in their pursuit. Of course, the Cocker's coat, which is the longest of the sporting spaniel coats, can be a hindrance in the field. So hunting enthusiasts often clip feathering to a manageable length.

Breed Description

Over the years, while devoted hunters began to favor other spaniel breeds in the field, the Cocker became increasingly popular as a show dog and family pet. The ideal height for a male dog is 15 inches (39 cm) and 14 inches (36 cm) for a female. Although weight is not defined in the breed standard, males tend to weigh between 24 and 28 pounds (10.8–12.6 kg) and females between 18 and 22 pounds (8.1–9.9 kg). Coats should be silky, flat, or slightly wavy. Excessive coat or one

This Cocker pup demonstrates its birdiness at an early age.

with a curly or cottony texture is considered undesirable. The Cocker's head and eyes are round, its ears long and pendulous, characteristics that contribute to an overall sweet expression and appearance.

A well-feathered, glamorous coat found in many colors is prized in the show ring. In fact, today the Cocker is divided into three coat color varieties that are shown separately: Solid Black (which includes Black and Tan), ASCOB (Any Solid Color Other than Black), and Parti-Color (two or more solid colors, one of which must be white). For more details see the breed standard at the end of the chapter.

Personality

Cocker Spaniels are a nice combination of sporting dog and lapdog rolled into one. They're hardy enough to enjoy long walks and romps as well as participate in a myriad of canine sports. But they're

A trio of attractive Cockers.

also light enough to pick up and carry or lounge comfortably in their owners' laps.

The Adaptable Cocker

Cockers are also very adaptable. They can live just as easily in an apartment as on a country estate. Generally speaking, these smallest of the sporting spaniels are happy and affectionate dogs. However, there are some personality differences linked to coat color. ASCOB's, except for chocolates that can be skittish, tend to be the most laid back of the three. Parti-colors are excitable, clownish, and usually more gregarious with other dogs. The solid blacks, which consistently win in obedience trials, seem to be the brightest though they can be domineering as well.

Regardless of coat color, all well-bred Cockers should display a merry temperament. And that they do. These little bundles of energy are outgoing tail waggers full of mischief. They love to play with toys, tear at tissues, and carry personal items belonging to their owners. The latter trait is shared with several of their spaniel cousins.

The Cocker as a Family Dog

Cockers simply adore family members and crave constant companionship. They're also easily excited by their people. One tricolor, Kiss, becomes quite wound up when her owner calls her name several times in fast succession. She runs in circles, going faster and faster, then suddenly takes off charging through the house.

True snuggle bunnies, Cockers love to be cuddled. If their owners leave the house, these spaniels are ecstatic when they return. They'll spring into their person's lap, bop them with a kiss, stand on their heads, then suddenly flip over with paws batting the air in a zillion directions. It's quite a greeting.

Agile dogs with great flexibility, Cockers seem able to contort themselves in the most uncomfortable-looking positions. Laying on their stomachs with back legs splayed out like a frog is a popular pose. They're also great leapers. It's not uncommon to see Cockers happily catapult into their owners arms after performing in an obedience or agility trial.

While Cockers are energetic and delight in playful activity, they can also keep pace with their owners' moods. If watching TV or reading a book is in order, a Cocker will lay nearby and take a nap. They will also snooze during the workday while their people are away, but need plenty of attention in the evening.

Breed Characteristics

Despite all of the breed's wonderful attributes, first-time owners are often dismayed to find the Cocker personality isn't quite what they were expecting. For example, buff female Cockers are highly sought after. Because of the attractive golden tresses, puppy buyers have the mistaken notion these spaniels are miniature Golden Retrievers. But

A Black and Tan Cocker plays King of the Hill.

in reality, their temperaments are not at all similar. Goldens are large, mellow dogs with a very strong desire to please their people. They make wonderful family pets because they take having their ears pulled and being ridden like a pony along with other childish pranks in stride. Cockers have feistier dispositions. They are less tolerant and forgiving of roughhousing.

That bold, confident manner, a "look at me, I'm terrific" attitude, wins points in the show ring, but it can also spell trouble in the home of an inexperienced owner. If their place in the family pack is not clearly established, Cockers of any color may take over the house. Growling or refusing to get off furniture or not allowing their people to pass through a doorway are just some of the inappropriate behaviors that may take place. On the other end of the spectrum are shy and submissive Cockers. These dogs lack confidence and may wet every time someone comes to the door, or worse, bite out of fear.

The Disadvantages of Demand

As mentioned earlier, Cocker Spaniels have enjoyed longer-lasting popularity than any other breed. Over the years, reputable breeders worked diligently to preserve the Cocker's original endearing qualities. They spent a good deal of time researching the genetics of the dogs they intend to breed, paying close attention to health and temperament problems, making every effort to avoid passing along negative traits. Unfortunately, the unprecedented demand for Cockers in the 1930s to 1950s brought a surge in puppy mills and backyard breeders. Puppy mills are large commercial operations that breed dogs for profit, giving little thought to temperament or health conditions. Quantity is more important than quality. Backyard breeders are inexperienced people casually mating two dogs of the same breed without considering their genetic makeup. Although these dogs may be raised in a home environment, their health and temperament problems are often the same. As a result, Cockers of inappropriate size who exhibited shy or snappish temperaments and suffered various types of health problems became all too common.

Those devoted to the breed have tried to overcome the problems of the past and have in many ways been successful. It is possible to find

The Cocker Spaniel's luxurious coat requires regular grooming.

a healthy, well-bred Cocker with the merry, friendly temperament it should possess. But it does take effort on the part of the prospective owner to find a suitable pet. This can be done by contacting several breeders, discussing health and temperament problems in their lines, and meeting as many dogs as possible before making a selection.

Making the Cocker Commitment

It should be noted even a well-bred Cocker can exhibit unacceptable behavior if improperly cared for. Cockers have a profuse coat that requires regular grooming. Owners must enjoy this task themselves or be committed to having their dogs professionally groomed every four to six weeks with at-home combings between visits. If grooming is neglected, particularly around the ears, Cockers can develop ear infections and mats the size of golf balls. Those involved in Cocker rescue receive numerous dogs in terrible condition and many are surly and snappish simply because they are in pain.

Some pet owners prefer to keep coats clipped short leaving some feathering on the chest and legs. This is an acceptable option with two caveats. Dogs should be accustomed to having their coats cut short at an early age, as clipping down an adult Cocker can be traumatic for the dog. Also, be aware once a coat is trimmed with electric clippers it will never grow back to its original silky texture.

A buff Cocker shoots out of a tunnel in agility.

Temperament

Because Cockers are adaptable, they make good pets for seniors as well as families with older considerate children. Cockers are not recommended for homes with preschoolers, as they just aren't cut out for the rough handling very young children often bestow upon pets.

These spaniels make fine watchdogs. They're protective of their homes and property and will bark an incessant alarm if visitors or intruders are on the grounds. They warm up easily to company, often displaying the same enthusiastic greeting given their owners. However, some are more reserved and greet strangers at a less frenetic pace. On the whole, Cockers get along with other dogs and animals. Sometimes new dog acquaintances are exasperated by their playful enthusiasm.

Cocker pups require a good deal of socialization—puppy kindergarten classes are wonderful—to develop the confident, merry temperament they are meant to have.

Training

Cocker Spaniels are intelligent dogs that respond fairly well to training. Some fanciers believe their dogs are anxious to please them. Others feel the breed has more of a "what's in it for me" attitude. Housebreaking can take a while, and it's not unusual for adult Cockers to have lapses in their training.

Sensitive dogs, these spaniels will not tolerate harsh training methods. They'll refuse to cooperate if treated unfairly. They can also be stubborn if they're just not in the mood to mind. The breed does have an intense food drive, however, so using bits of frozen liver, pieces of hot dog, or other goodies as a motivator reaps very positive results in the early stages of training. It works well with adults too, though at least one obedience Cocker displayed some cunning behavior in this regard.

After earning her UD, Pearl, a black and tan became ring-wise. She was working toward her UDX, which requires two "go outs." During this exercise, the dog must run a certain distance beyond its trainer on command and wait to be sent over a jump. In practice, Pearl was always rewarded for her properly executed go outs. However, food is not allowed during a licensed trial. She ran well on her first go out, but on the second she ran halfway, then stopped and stared at her owner with a look that clearly read, "didn't you forget something?" She then refused to complete the exercise.

Obedience and Agility Trials

Generally, Cocker Spaniels are not seen as frequently in trials as some of the popular obedience breeds. Though, of course, almost any dog given the right time and devotion can be successful in this sport. Cockers bore easily with repetition and often like to put their own spin on things. During the heeling exercise in an obedience trial, one clever female decided the tape holding the floor mat down made an interesting little jump and hopped over it.

Cockers are also very attentive to their owners and in tune to their moods. If a trainer gets the jitters in the ring, a Cocker may well mirror that nervous energy.

Many Cockers are natural retrievers. Most have excellent noses. One particular female was able to locate and retrieve the very rock her owner tossed to the bottom of a lake. She could also find her plastic banana buried in snow and smell her Christmas goodies hidden 15 feet above her head. With those scenting abilities, it's not surprising Cockers do well in the sport of tracking.

Agile dogs with lots of energy, Cockers love the excitement of agility and also excel in this sport. But their stars truly shine in the show ring. Friendly enough to be shuttled back and forth between their owners, handlers, and groomers, they take to the ring with pizazz. A great attitude combined with chiseled features and glamorous coats make for a winning combination.

Exercise and Grooming

Cocker Spaniels do not require as much hard exercise as some of their relatives. A good daily walk and weekly romp in a safe area should keep a Cocker fit. The breed tends to self-exercise when given the opportunity, so an enclosed yard can take the place of walks.

Although Cockers will delight in playing ball until their owners are worn out, they are just as happy to laze around the house. However, this couch potato aspect of their personality coupled with an enormous food drive can contribute to unhealthy weight gain if not given moderate exercise on a routine basis.

Small though they are, keep in mind Cockers are sporting dogs. Therefore, mental stimulation is just as important as a physical outlet. A bored Cocker will surely find its way into trouble.

Coat

The importance of routinely grooming a Cocker Spaniel cannot be overemphasized. The silky coat mats easily if not properly cared for. After a Cocker is spayed or neutered, the coat develops a cottony texture and becomes more profuse, which increases the likelihood of matting.

Pets should be brushed and combed down to the skin several times a week. Daily is even better. A bath and trim is in order every four to six weeks. Clippers can be used on the head, face, neck, and ears, and topside of the paws. The hair under the tail and between the toes should be trimmed with scissors. The other option is to trim the coat with a number-ten blade, leaving a slight fringe on the legs while still neatening the head, tail, and feet.

Grooming show dogs is even more laborious. Daily combing is required, along with a bath and trim every two weeks. The body can never be clipped. Most exhibitors strip (pluck individual hairs) by hand or with a stripping knife.

Trick or Treat.

Breed-Specific Health Concerns

Cocker Spaniels have been besieged with health problems. Some are relatively minor and easy to control, others are life threatening. Many conditions involve the eyes and include cataracts, cherry eye, conjunctivitis, dry eye, glaucoma, and progressive retinal atrophy.

Cockers are also prone to various skin conditions, including ear infections, lipfold pyoderma, infections of the lipfold, and seborrhea.

Of a more serious nature are two kidney conditions: familial renal disease and congenital hypoplasia. Both cause improper kidney growth and shorten life span. Autoimmune diseases (when the tissue of the body attacks itself) and resultant allergies have affected the breed.

Epilepsy and hip dysplasia are other health concerns, though they occur less frequently than some of the other conditions. All puppy buyers need to be aware of potential health problems before buying a family pet, but it is particularly important in researching Cocker Spaniels. Be sure to deal with reputable breeders willing to discuss potential health concerns.

Official Standard

General Appearance

The Cocker Spaniel is the smallest member of the Sporting Group. He has a sturdy, compact body and a cleanly chiseled and refined head, with the overall dog in complete balance and of ideal size. He stands well up at the shoulder on straight forelegs with a topline sloping slightly toward strong, moderately bent, muscular quarters. He is a dog capable of considerable speed, combined with great endurance. Above all, he must be free and merry, sound, well balanced throughout and in action show a keen inclination to work. A dog well balanced in all parts is more desirable than a dog with strongly contrasting good points and faults.

Size, Proportion, Substance

Size: The ideal height at the withers for an adult dog is 15 inches and for an adult bitch, 14 inches. Height may vary one-half inch above or below this ideal. A dog whose height exceeds 15½ inches or a bitch whose height exceeds 14½ inches shall be disqualified. An adult dog whose height is less than 14½ inches and an adult bitch whose height is less than 13½ inches shall be penalized. Height is determined by a line perpendicular to the ground from the top of the shoulder blades, the dog standing naturally with its forelegs and lower hind legs parallel to the line of measurement.

Proportion: The measurement from the breast bone to back of thigh is slightly longer than the measurement from the highest point of withers to the ground. The body must be of sufficient length to permit a straight and free stride; the dog never appears long and low.

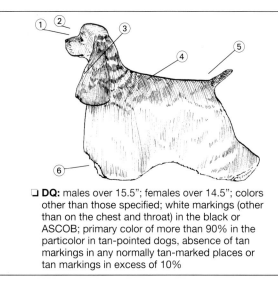

Illustrated Standard

① Expression alert, soft, and appealing
② Rounded skull with pronounced stop
③ Long, low-set, lobular ears
④ Topline slopes slightly to rear
⑤ Tail docked and carried in line or slightly higher than the topline
⑥ Round feet

❏ **Color:** Black variety: solid black or black and tan; ASCOB variety: any solid color other than black, including cream, red, brown, and brown with tan points; Particolor variety: any of the allowed solid colors broken up on a white background; also roans

❏ **DQ:** males over 15.5"; females over 14.5"; colors other than those specified; white markings (other than on the chest and throat) in the black or ASCOB; primary color of more than 90% in the particolor in tan-pointed dogs, absence of tan markings in any normally tan-marked places or tan markings in excess of 10%

Head

To attain a well-proportioned head, which must be in balance with the rest of the dog, it embodies the following:

Expression: The expression is intelligent, alert, soft and appealing.

Eyes: Eyeballs are round and full and look directly forward. The shape of the eye rims gives a slightly almond shaped appearance; the eye is not weak or goggled. The color of the iris is dark brown and in general the darker the better.

Ears: Lobular, long, of fine leather, well feathered, and placed no higher than a line to the lower part of the eye.

Skull: Rounded but not exaggerated with no tendency toward flatness; the eyebrows are clearly defined with a pronounced stop. The bony structure beneath the eyes is well chiseled with no prominence in the cheeks. The muzzle is broad and deep, with square even jaws. To be in correct balance, the distance from the stop to the tip of the nose is one half the distance from the stop up over the crown to the base of the skull.

Nose: Of sufficient size to balance the muzzle and foreface, with well-developed nostrils typical of a sporting dog. It is black in color in the blacks, black and tans, and black and whites; in other colors it may be brown, liver, or black, the darker the better. The color of nose harmonizes with the color of the eye rim.

Lips: The upper lip is full and of sufficient depth to cover the lower jaw.

Teeth: Teeth strong and sound, not too small and meet in a scissors bite.

63

Neck, Topline, Body

Neck: The neck is sufficiently long to allow the nose to reach the ground easily, muscular and free from pendulous "throatiness." It rises strongly from the shoulders and arches slightly as it tapers to join the head.

Topline: Sloping slightly toward muscular quarters.

Body: The chest is deep, its lowest point no higher than the elbows, its front sufficiently wide for adequate heart and lung space, yet not so wide as to interfere with the straightforward movement of the forelegs. Ribs are deep and well sprung. Back is strong and sloping evenly and slightly downward from the shoulders to the set-on of the docked tail. The docked tail is set on and carried on a line with the topline of the back, or slightly higher; never straight up like a Terrier and never so low as to indicate timidity. When the dog is in motion the tail action is merry.

Forequarters

The shoulders are well laid back forming an angle with the upper arm of approximately 90 degrees, which permits the dog to move his forelegs in an easy manner with forward reach. Shoulders are clean-cut and sloping without protrusion and so set that the upper points of the withers are at an angle which permits a wide spring of rib. When viewed from the side with the forelegs vertical, the elbow is directly below the highest point of the shoulder blade. Forelegs are parallel, straight, strongly boned and muscular and set close to the body well under the scapulae. The pasterns are short and strong. Dewclaws on forelegs may be removed. Feet compact, large, round, and firm with horny pads; they turn neither in nor out.

Hindquarters

Hips are wide and quarters well rounded and muscular. When viewed from behind, the hind legs are parallel when in motion and at rest. The hind legs are strongly boned and muscled with moderate angulation at the stifle and powerful, clearly defined thighs. The stifle is strong and there is no slippage of it in motion or when standing. The hocks are strong and well let down. Dewclaws on hind legs may be removed.

Coat

On the head, short and fine; on the body, medium length, with enough undercoating to give protection. The ears, chest, abdomen, and legs are well feathered, but not so excessively as to hide the Cocker Spaniel's true lines and movement or affect his appearance and function as a moderately coated sporting dog. The texture is most important. The coat is silky, flat, or slightly wavy and of a texture which permits easy care. Excessive coat or curly- or cottony-textured coat shall be severely penalized. Use of electric clippers on the back coat is not desirable. Trimming to enhance the dog's true lines should be done to appear as natural as possible.

Color and Markings

Black Variety: Solid color black to include black with tan points. The black should be jet; shadings of brown or liver in the coat are not desirable. A small amount of white on the chest and/or throat is allowed; white in any other location shall disqualify.

Any Solid Color Other than Black (ASCOB): Any solid color other than black, ranging from lightest cream to darkest red, including brown and brown with tan points. The color shall be of a uniform shade, but lighter color of the feathering is permissible. A small amount of white on the chest and/or throat is allowed; white in any other location shall disqualify.

Parti-Color Variety: Two or more solid, well-broken colors, one of which must be white; black and white, red and white (the red may range from lightest cream to darkest red), brown and white, and roans, to include any such color combination with tan points. It is preferable that the tan markings be located in the same pattern as for the tan points in the Black and ASCOB varieties. Roans are classified as parti-colors and may be of any of the usual roaning patterns. Primary color which is ninety percent (90%) or more shall disqualify.

Tan Points: The color of the tan may be from the lightest cream to the darkest red and is restricted to ten percent (10%) or less of the color of the specimen; tan markings in excess of that amount shall disqualify. In the case of tan points in the Black or ASCOB variety, the markings shall be located as follows:

1. A clear tan spot over each eye;

2. On the sides of the muzzle and on the cheeks;

3. On the underside of the ears;

4. On all feet and/or legs;

5. Under the tail;

6. On the chest, optional; presence or absence shall not be penalized.

Tan markings which are not readily visible or which amount only to traces, shall be penalized. Tan on the muzzle which extends upward, over and joins shall also be penalized. The absence of tan markings in the Black or ASCOB variety in any of the specified locations in any otherwise tan-pointed dog shall disqualify.

Gait

The Cocker Spaniel, though the smallest of the sporting dogs, possesses a typical sporting dog gait. Prerequisite to good movement is balance between the front and rear assemblies. He drives with strong, powerful rear quarters and is properly constructed in the shoulders and forelegs so that he can reach forward without constriction in a full stride to counterbalance the driving force from the rear. Above all, his gait is coordinated, smooth, and effortless. The dog must cover ground with his action; excessive animation should not be mistaken for proper gait.

Temperament

Equable in temperament with no suggestion of timidity.

Disqualifications

Height: Males over 15½ inches; females over 14½ inches.

Color and Markings: The aforementioned colors are the only acceptable colors or combination of colors. Any other colors or combination of colors to disqualify.

Black Variety: White markings except on chest and throat.

Any Solid Color Other than Black Variety: White markings except on chest and throat.

Parti-Color Variety: Primary color ninety percent (90%) or more.

Tan Points: (1) Tan markings in excess of ten percent (10%); (2) Absence of tan markings in Black or ASCOB Variety in any of the specified locations in an otherwise tan pointed dog.

Approved May 12, 1992
Effective June 30, 1992
© 1997 by the American Kennel Club.
Courtesy of the American Spaniel Club, Inc.

Chapter Seven

The English Cocker Spaniel

History

Hearing the key in the door, she sails off the couch, eyes gleaming with pleasure, long silky ears flying through the air. As her mistress enters the room, she wiggles and squirms, tail all aflutter while her dainty paws dance upon the floor. Nearly gurgling with delight after a few quick kisses, she leaps back onto the couch ready for their afternoon snuggle. Who could resist a greeting like that? The English Cocker Spaniel's sweet expression and merry disposition would surely melt the most hardened heart.

Because Cocker Spaniels are one of the most popular dogs in the country, many dog lovers aren't aware of the fact there are actually two Cocker breeds: Cocker Spaniels and English Cocker Spaniels. The latter are often referred to as ECs or Engies by fanciers. Whereas Cockers ranked number 13 in 1998 with 34,632 registrations, English Cockers ranked number 77 with only 1,174 registrations.

Origin of the Breed

Early in their history, Cockers and English Cockers were frequently interbred much to the dismay of devotees of either type. Then in 1935, The English Cocker Spaniel Club of America was formed to sort out the confusion and purify the English Cocker strain. Much of the credit for accomplishing this monumental task belongs to Geraldine Rockefeller Dodge. Then president of the club and a staunch dog fancier, she imported only the best English Cocker specimens from Europe for her breeding program, and initiated extensive pedigree research. Eventually, the two types were segregated and improved. In 1946, the English Cocker Spaniel was recognized by the AKC as a distinct breed. Over the years, in the United States, English Cockers have not achieved the same popularity as Cockers. On the other hand, neither have they suffered the pitfalls that too much popularity often brings. In Europe, however, they are the best known and most numerous spaniels.

The Breed Today

Breed Description

English Cockers are slightly larger and heavier than Cockers. The English Cocker ranges in height from 15 to 17 inches (39–44 cm) and weighs between 26 and 34 pounds (11.7–15.3 kg) as compared to its cousin, which stands between 14 and 15 inches (36–39 cm) and weighs between 18 and 28 pounds (8.1–12.6 kg). English Cockers give a leggier appearance and have larger, longer, setterlike muzzles. The Cocker's head is rounder and has quite a bit more feathering overall.

English Cockers can be found in a variety of colors: sixty percent of the population are blue roan, which is black spots on a white background

A field-bred English Cocker Spaniel.

laced with black hairs. The resulting appearance ranges from silver to a near solid black. Twenty percent are black or varying shades of red. The remaining twenty percent are black and white, liver and white, black/white and tan, liver/white and tan, blue roan and tan, liver roan, liver roan and tan, orange and white, orange roan, black and tan, solid liver, and liver and tan.

The ideal English Cocker coat is flat and silky (though some coats are wavy) and of medium length with moderately long feathering on the ears, chest, belly and backs of the front and rear legs.

Originally bred for hunting fowl and rabbits that often lie hidden in dense cover, English Cockers are eager hunters. Their short bodies and strong legs make them capable of great speed, and they seem to have endless stamina. These hearty little spaniels are one of the breeds that have divided into two types: show-bred and field-bred. A division in form and function takes place when field trials and conformation shows are made available for a particular breed. Fanciers usually strive for perfection in one arena and cater their breeding programs toward raising pups that will excel in that area. For example, the longer silky coat may win raves in the ring, but it will surely slow the hunting dog down.

Field-bred English Cockers look quite a bit different from their show-bred counterparts. They are generally smaller dogs, with much shorter coats. Their heads are less elegantly shaped and their tails, though also docked, are longer.

When Cocker field trials were held in this country from 1924 to 1965, field-breds were frequently imported from England. After the trials were discontinued, interest in these superb gun dogs also waned. Today, there are some field-bred breeders around, but their numbers are few.

Interestingly, many show-bred English Cockers still retain their hunting abilities. A good percentage would make fine gun dogs for the weekend hunter. These capable Cockers still have the nose, desire, and instinct. However, they lack the drive and stamina of the field breds.

Because of their stature, English Cockers are specialists in plowing through or under cover unlike some of the larger breeds who tend to leap over underbrush. They are extremely adept at flushing woodcock, a type of game that stays well hidden and will not take flight until absolutely necessary. A Springer, for example, moving at breakneck speed and flying over cover, could miss a woodcock, whereas the English Cocker can just as easily root it out.

English Cockers also have a soft, cautious flush, as opposed to hard-flushing dogs who slam into an area where game lies, quickly rousting it into the air. A busy, methodical worker, the English Cocker's tail is always in motion and speeds up when it catches the scent.

Interest in field-trialing Cockers has grown in recent years. In 1993, these rigorous competitions were

Double Trouble.

reestablished. Perhaps twenty percent of our modern show-bred English Cockers would have the ability to successfully compete.

Personality

The English Cocker's somewhat solemn looks belie its cheerful nature. These are happy little dogs as evidenced by their incessantly wagging tails. They are very eager to take part in family activities. In fact, they expect to be included and can't understand why separation from those they love is sometimes necessary. Although they can tolerate being left alone during the workday, if lavished with attention in the evening, they will thrive if someone is home part of the time.

These spaniels are very adaptable dogs. Though truly in their element in the country, they adjust easily to urban life if given adequate exercise. They fit in with any lifestyle and make equally good companions for the elderly or the young sportsman.

Temperament

There does seem to be a wide variety in temperament however. Some English Cockers are quiet, mellow dogs whereas others are very busy, noisy, and even pesty. So if possible, it's best for prospective English Cocker owners to meet with several breeders and observe their dogs' behaviors. It's also a good idea to discuss lifestyle and what is expected from an English Cocker. Obviously, the higher-energy dogs would make better pets for active families or those interested in participating in canine performance events.

English Cockers love to explore.

English Cockers of all temperaments are loving and affectionate. They live to snuggle and because of their small size are light enough to scoop up in one's arms. These endearing dogs just seem to spill into their owners laps and are easy to hug and cuddle. They tend to cling to those they love by following them around the house and always seem to be underfoot.

The Desire for Food

English Cockers also live to eat and are very intense about their desire for food. Once Jemma, a blue roan and tan, passed by a table of food en route to an agility class. She began the course, leaping over the first jump and scrambling up the A-frame. Then she stopped, looked at her owner, and raced away passing several groups of people and dogs. Moments later she sailed into the air and landed squarely in the middle of the food table!

Another mischievous pup always poked her head and body into the refrigerator every time it was opened. One day she was inadvertently locked inside. Minutes later her frantic owner opened the door and discovered the unperturbed pup on the lower shelf happily munching on an apple.

Many fanciers have witnessed their dogs in an apparent quest to "dig to China" to reach a crumb that's fallen behind the fridge. These little characters easily become overweight if fed too many treats. So English Cocker owners must steel themselves against those melting, pleading eyes.

Breed Characteristics

Fun-loving and curious, English Cockers are busy dogs and enjoy exploring, whether it be their own backyards or the neighborhood park. They're also very adept at inventing their own games like bouncing a tennis ball by themselves or shredding tissue and paper. And they're always ready for a good time. They'll bound joyfully into the house, leap on the couch, and instantly fall asleep. If awakened, they're ready and eager for more fun and games.

These sweet-natured spaniels love people. Some are a little reserved with strangers at first, especially on their own property, but after a few minutes will smother the newcomer with kisses. Others are demonstrative from the moment of introduction. They seem to have a special affinity for children and delight in their company. Of course, children must treat these dogs with care. Too much roughhousing might overwhelm a thirty-pound spaniel.

Merlin, a red English Cocker, loved to visit youngsters at a children's shelter. A sweet-natured dog with a great desire to fetch and retrieve, he was a very popular pet therapist. One little boy was particularly enamored with Merlin. He managed to bring the dog onto the playground equipment and later offered to buy him for all the money he possessed in the world— $2.00.

English Cockers usually get along well with their own kind. Though not outwardly aggressive with dogs, they will defend themselves if threat-

ECs have a special affinity for children.

ened. They're quite curious about other animals, especially small furry or feathered beings, and can't resist a good game of chase. However, they don't seem inclined to want to harm anyone. If a small animal is caught, an English Cocker tends to carry it around gently or offer the creature to its owner. These spaniels can be taught to respect (i.e., ignore) pet rabbits and birds and still do well in the field.

English Cockers are wonderful watchdogs. They readily alert their owners to the arrival of uninvited guests. If several of these spaniels live together, they will set up a "point man" to run out ahead of the others while the entire pack barks an alarm. They're unlikely to bite, however, and would never be considered guard dogs.

Easygoing, loyal, and demonstrative, English Cockers are not without

A red male and his pup.

Most of these negative traits can be curbed with proper training and attention, though there's not much one can do about the sloppy water habits other than to "grin and bear it."

English Cockers are very bright dogs and continually surprise their owners with their ingenuity. They've been known to pop the tops off of cans, unbolt crates, and open doors. Obviously, this is a breed that needs to have its energy and intelligence properly channeled. They enjoy having a job to do, whether it be performing in a sport or being helpful around the house. One English Cocker owner has trained her dog to bring a pair of glasses to another member of the family. This same fancier claims English Cockers are addictive. Surely acting as the voice of many, she warns prospective owners with a smile, "if you get one, plan on having more."

their shortcomings. For some dog owners, the high energy is too much energy and can be annoying. Less heavily coated than Cockers, English Cockers have their fair share of feathers, and many shed heavily. They require regular and somewhat time-consuming grooming to look their best.

Some are very sloppy with their water habits—a trait shared with Clumber and Field Spaniels. After taking a drink, water dribbles from their mouths and ear feathers as they go along their merry way.

English Cockers are frequently jealous of attention and possessive of their toys. Their food drive can lead to garbage stealing and pestiness for treats. Though they like to keep themselves clean by wiping their faces on carpeting and licking their paws, they're also known to break their house training.

Training

Although most English Cockers are eager to please their owners, many have a stubborn streak. They can be difficult to house-train initially, and as mentioned earlier may break their training as adults.

English Cockers learn other lessons fairly quickly, but they have independent minds and try to do things their own way. They will test their owners and can rule the house if pack leadership is not established early on.

These capable little spaniels are not specialists in the field of sports. They can do it all. They make excellent show dogs with their array of coat colors and snappy looks. They're very portable on the campaign trail, though they require a good deal of grooming. Many English Cocker fanciers purchase these dogs with an eye toward the show ring.

Because of their intelligence, they can do well in obedience. However, they bore easily with repetition and can get turned off. They're also soft dogs who will shut down if treated with a heavy hand. Owners must be clever with their training techniques, making the exercises fun for the dog. Motivating with food rewards works well with English Cockers.

Most English Cockers would probably prefer agility or flyball. They excel at these sports due to their size and athleticism. Of course, if English Cocker owners really want to make their canine companions happy, they should take them tracking. Because of their hunting prowess and keen noses, they love to track and do so with great zeal.

Exercise and Grooming

Obviously, English Cockers, especially adolescents, are energetic dogs. A daily exercise program is necessary to keep them physically and mentally fit. Long walks, games of fetch, and field work are ideal.

Many English Cockers tend to self-exercise if they have access to a safe, enclosed yard, though they will certainly enjoy company in their athletic pursuits.

Because these Cockers are notorious "chow hounds," they will develop weight problems if their exercise requirements are neglected.

Coat

Properly grooming an English Cocker is time-consuming, but most pet owners can learn to do it themselves if given instruction. English Cockers have long guard hairs on top of their bodies with soft undercoats. They should be brushed out

A 12-year-old boy grooms an English Cocker for the show ring.

once a week—daily during shedding season in the spring and fall. Clippers can be used on the body of pet dogs. The face, ears, tail, and feet will also need to be trimmed. Feathering can be kept long or shortened.

Care of the show dog is more involved. The body is never clipped but rather stripped, which means plucking tufts of hair with the hands or a stripping knife and grooming stone.

English Cocker owners may opt to use a professional groomer. But it's important to find one who is familiar with the proper English Cocker grooming style. Whether done at home or by a professional, English Cockers should be fully groomed every six to eight weeks in addition to weekly brushing and baths as needed. Show dogs are bathed and groomed more frequently.

Breed-Specific Health Concerns

Because English Cockers have not been overbred, they do not suffer as many or as frequent health problems as their American cousins. However, there are a few genetic disorders known to occur. Like many of the long-eared spaniels, they are prone to ear infections. They have also been known to suffer from progressive retinal atrophy, epilepsy, two renal diseases (congenital hypoplasia and familial renal disease), and to some extent hip dysplasia, which is usually more significant in larger breeds.

There has been some incidence of congenital deafness in English Cockers. A computerized test known as the Baer Test is available to ascertain degree of hearing loss.

Official Standard

General Appearance

The English Cocker Spaniel is an active, merry sporting dog, standing well up at the withers and compactly built. He is alive with energy; his gait is powerful and frictionless, capable both of covering ground effortlessly and penetrating dense cover to flush and retrieve game. His enthusiasm in the field and the incessant action of his tail while at work indicate how much he enjoys the hunting for which he was bred. His head is especially characteristic. He is, above all, a dog of balance, both standing and moving, without exaggeration in any part, the whole worth more than the sum of its parts.

Size, Proportion, Substance

Size: Height at withers: males 16 to 17 inches; females 15 to 16 inches. Deviations to be penalized. The most desirable weights: males, 28 to 34 pounds; females, 26 to 32 pounds. Proper conformation and substance should be considered more important than weight alone.

Proportion: Compactly built and short-coupled, with height at withers slightly greater than the distance from withers to set-on of tail.

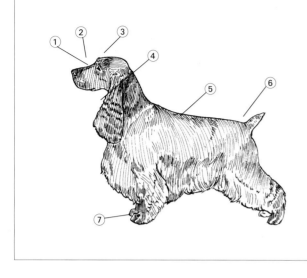

Substance: The English Cocker is a solidly built dog with as much bone and substance as is possible without becoming cloddy or coarse.

Head

General appearance: strong, yet free from coarseness, softly contoured, without sharp angles. Taken as a whole, the parts combine to produce the expression distinctive of the breed.

Expression: Soft, melting, yet dignified, alert, and intelligent.

Eyes: The eyes are essential to the desired expression. They are medium in size, full and slightly oval; set wide apart; lids tight. Haws are inconspicuous; may be pigmented or unpigmented. Eye color dark brown, except in livers and liver parti-colors where hazel is permitted, but the darker the hazel the better.

Ears: Set low, lying close to the head; leather fine, extending to the nose, well covered with long, silky, straight or slightly wavy hair.

Skull: Arched and slightly flattened when seen both from the side and from the front. Viewed in profile, the brow appears not appreciably higher than the back-skull. Viewed from above, the sides of the skull are in planes roughly parallel to those of the muzzle. Stop definite, but moderate, and slightly grooved.

Muzzle: Equal in length to skull; well cushioned; only as much narrower than the skull as is consistent with a full eye placement; cleanly chiseled under the eyes. Jaws strong, capable of carrying game. Nostrils wide for proper development of scenting ability; color black, except in livers and parti-colors of that shade where they will be brown; reds and parti-colors of that shade may be brown, but black is preferred. Lips square, but not pendulous or showing prominent flews.

Bite: Scissors. A level bite is not preferred. Overshot or undershot to be severely penalized.

Neck, Topline and Body

Neck: Graceful and muscular, arched toward the head and blending cleanly, without throatiness, into sloping shoulders; moderate in length and in balance with the length and height of the dog.

Topline: The line of the neck blends into the shoulder and backline in a smooth curve. The backline slopes very slightly toward a gently rounded croup, and is free from sagging or rumpiness.

Body: Compact and well-knit, giving the impression of strength without heaviness. Chest deep; not so wide as to interfere with action of forelegs, nor so narrow as to allow the front to appear narrow or pinched. Forechest well developed, prosternum projecting moderately beyond shoulder points. Brisket reaches to the elbow and slopes gradually to a moderate tuck-up. Ribs well sprung and springing gradually to mid-body, tapering to back ribs which are of good depth and extend well back. Back short and strong. Loin short, broad and very slightly arched, but not enough to affect the topline appreciably. Croup gently rounded, without any tendency to fall away sharply.

Tail: Docked. Set on to conform to croup. Ideally, the tail is carried horizontally and is in constant motion while the dog is in action. Under excitement, the dog may carry his tail somewhat higher, but not cocked up.

Forequarters

The English Cocker is moderately angulated. Shoulders are sloping, the blade flat and smoothly fitting. Shoulder blade and upper arm are approximately equal in length. Upper arm set well back, joining the shoulder with sufficient angulation to place the elbow beneath the highest point of the shoulder blade when the dog is standing naturally.

Forelegs: Straight, with bone nearly uniform in size from elbow to heel; elbows set close to the body; pasterns nearly straight, with some flexibility.

Feet: Proportionate in size to the legs, firm, round and catlike; toes arched and tight; pads thick.

Hindquarters

Angulation moderate and, most importantly, in balance with that of the forequarters. Hips relatively broad and well rounded. Upper thighs broad, thick and muscular, providing plenty of propelling power. Second thighs well muscled and approximately equal in length to the upper. Stifle strong and well bent. Hock to pad short. Feet as in front.

Coat

On head, short and fine; of medium length on body; flat or slightly wavy; silky in texture. The English Cocker is well-feathered, but not so profusely as to interfere with field work. Trimming is permitted to remove overabundant hair and to enhance the dog's true lines. It should be done so as to appear as natural as possible.

Color

Various. Parti-colors are either clearly marked, ticked or roaned, the white appearing in combination with black, liver or shades of red. In parti-colors it is preferable that solid markings be broken on the body and more or less evenly distributed; absence of body markings is acceptable. Solid colors are black, liver or shades of red. White feet on a solid are undesirable; a little white on throat is acceptable; but in neither case do these white markings make the dog a parti-color. Tan markings, clearly defined and of rich shade, may appear in conjunction with black, livers and parti-color combinations of those colors. Black and tans and liver and tans are considered solid colors.

Gait

The English Cocker is capable of hunting in dense cover and upland terrain. His gait is accordingly characterized more by drive and the appearance of power than by great speed. He covers ground effortlessly and with extension both in front and in rear, appropriate to his angulation. In the ring, he carries his head proudly and is able to keep much the same topline while in action as when standing for examination. Going and coming, he moves in a straight line without crabbing or rolling, and with width between both front and rear legs appropriate to his build and gait.

Temperament

The English Cocker is merry and affectionate, of equable disposition, neither sluggish nor hyperactive, a willing worker and a faithful and engaging companion.

Approved October 11, 1988
Effective November 30, 1988
© 1999 by the American Kennel Club.
Courtesy of the English Cocker
Spaniel Club of America, Inc.

Chapter Eight

The English Springer Spaniel

History

Zig, zag, forward, back, a blur of black and white ignites the field. Moments later the dog slams into the underbrush flushing his quarry. A vision to behold, as he performs the work he was bred for, this English Springer Spaniel is competing in a field trial.

Ringside, spectators hold their breath as another black and white spaniel makes a final pass in front of the judge. A majestic creature, his long silky coat seems to glide through the air, his paws barely touching the ground. The judge points in his direction. The crowds cheer. This English Springer has just finished his Championship of Record.

Origin of the Breed

The Springer got its name from its ability to flush "spring" game. Leggiest of the AKC-recognized flushing breeds, the English Springer Spaniel has long been the world's premier sporting spaniel, the dog by which all others are compared.

The British separated and recognized Cockers and Springers in 1902. The first English Springer was registered with the AKC in 1910. But it wasn't until 1924 that the English Springer Spaniel Field Trial Association (ESSFTA) was formed and became the parent club for the breed in the United States. The English Springer Spaniel actually gained popularity in Canada prior to catching on with dog fanciers in America. Eudore Chevrier of Winnipeg is credited with importing many fine English Springers from overseas and later exporting them to this country.

In the early years, the English Springer Spaniel could do it all—hunt and compete in the show ring. But as with the English Cocker, fanciers began to split their interests and breeding programs. Those intent on winning in field trials worked diligently to create a hard-driving hunting dog. Those who desired show champions concentrated on perfecting form rather than function. As a result two distinct types of Springers emerged, and the days of dual champions were over. The last dual championship was earned in the early 1940s.

The Breed Today

Today, the English Springer is the second most popular sporting spaniel. In 1998, 11,578 dogs were registered. The division between show-bred and field-bred types is so keen, they appear to be different breeds. However, the AKC does not differentiate between the two. And the ESSFA continues to represent both. Show-bred Springer males are generally twenty inches (52 cm) high and weigh about fifty pounds (22.5 kg). Females tend to be an inch (2.6 cm) shorter and roughly ten pounds (4.5 kg) lighter. Field-breds are less uniform in size but are usually smaller than the show-breds, though some have been as large as retrievers. Field-breds also have shorter ears and less coat, which is predominantly white with irregular patches of color and a good deal of ticking. Their flashier brothers generally sport a dark saddle across their backs against a white backdrop. Colors found in both are the same: liver and white, black and white, blue or liver roan, and tricolor, liver and white or black and white with tan markings above the eyebrows, on the cheeks, inside the ear, and under the tail. Both also have docked tails, though those on the working types are generally left longer with a furry flag on the tip.

The English Springer as a Hunter

Not surprisingly, field-bred Springers are supreme hunters. Best described as bundles of bottled energy that explode in the field, these spaniels are exceptional pheasant dogs. Covering ground at breakneck speed, they have a hard-driving flush that gives hidden game birds no other option but to take to the air. They're equally capable of staying on top of running birds until they too burst into flight. The field-breds tend to mature more rapidly both physically and mentally than other spaniels. They demonstrate their birdiness and retrieving instincts at a very early age.

Springer owners who hunt with their show-breds find they quarter, flush, and retrieve a little more calmly and with less flash and dash. Like their working counterparts, they're good on pheasant, quail, grouse, chukars, and woodcock. They can also handle their own retrieving waterfowl.

A field-bred English Springer Spaniel ignites the field.

The Energetic English Springer

English Springers are high-energy dogs—the field-breds obviously more so. Both must live in active households with a lot of opportunity to play and exercise. A fenced yard for safe running off leash is ideal. These dogs will also thrive if trained to participate in organized sports such as obedience, agility, and flyball. Either type can make fine pets, but field-breds will be happiest if given a chance to perform the work they were bred for.

While Springers are adaptable dogs and will adjust to urban life if given adequate exercise, they are probably too active for the elderly or those with sedentary lifestyles. A lack of exercise can lead to a myriad of annoying behavior problems, including destructive chewing and barking.

Personality

English Springers are known for their enthusiastic natures in everything they do. They take extreme pleasure in racing through fields and leaping into water. They're also eager to be included in other activities whether it be running an agility course or playing soccer with their "boy" and his pals. With bodies nearly coiled for action, they tend to bounce and spring in their antics.

Breed Characteristics

Indoors, these dogs are by no means couch potatoes. They can become restless if inclement weather or other causes interrupt their daily exercise routine. Springers also have an uncanny ability, as one fancier described it, to take a ten-minute "cat nap," then get up and run around with enough energy to light a small city. Or they can be sleeping, giving the impression they'll be sedate for a while, then suddenly jump up seeming to recall they left a toy in another room and race off to retrieve it.

Speaking of toys, Springers love to carry something around in their mouths. Some will go to sleep still grasping a treasured plaything. One male, Duncan, delights in holding onto his bone and playing with a ball at the same time.

A show-bred Springer strikes an aristocratic pose.

These spaniels are very affectionate with their people. They have a way of draping their bodies all over those they love—hugging and/or kissing all the while. They also have a tendency to sing—a distinctive "woo woo" when happy or expecting food.

English Springers can be excellent playmates for children if raised with them, and equally accepting of their friends. Of course, those who live in childless households may be wary of youngsters and prefer to keep their distance.

Generally, Springers enjoy the company of other dogs. They are eager to socialize with new canine acquaintances and can be very tolerant of each other. One female allowed puppies to hang on her ears, literally pulling her face to the ground. She stoically put up with their youthful antics and never complained.

If well socialized, English Springers can live in harmony with other pets. Many seem to have a particular affinity for cats. Of course, tolerance of pet birds may be expecting too much. Bird owners should always supervise interaction between their canine and feathered friends.

Like the other spaniel breeds, English Springers are good alarm barkers and offer some watch dog protection. However, their benign natures and loving outlook make them ineffectual guard dogs. While some may initially be reserved, the breed tends to be very accepting of new people. In fact, after being introduced one particular Springer,

This Springer executes a spectacular water entry.

Quark, takes strangers by the hand and leads them to the refrigerator!

A naturally curious dog, the English Springer Spaniel has a clownish streak. Toby, for example, likes to play tricks on his owner. A favorite is pretending a toy is stuck under the couch. He'll push his head underneath whining and barking until his mistress comes to investigate. After she realizes there's nothing there, Toby gleefully initiates a game of chase.

Well-bred English Springers have an infectious joie de vivre about them. They are enthusiastic, happy, and fun-loving. If given adequate outlets for their energy level, they're a delight to live with. Unfortunately, temperament problems have been known to occur in the breed. Some have exhibited dominance or fear aggression. These inappropriate behaviors have exhibited themselves around people and dogs. Others

Puppy love.

have demonstrated fits of Canine Rage—an affliction whereby a normally docile dog inexplicably attacks and later seems unaware of its behavior. The causes of Canine Rage have been hotly debated with no conclusive answer. Regardless, although the percentage of Springers who have had these fits is small and aggression in any form is wholly uncharacteristic for a properly-bred Springer, it is extremely important for prospective English Springer Spaniel buyers to deal with reputable breeders and discuss any questionable temperament problems in their line. Buyers should also meet the dam and sire of the pup they are considering as well as extended family members.

English Springers are wonderful companions for those who enjoy walking, hunting, or other active pursuits. They retain their youthful enthusiasm throughout their lives. However, this type of high energy may be too much exuberance for those who prefer a more sedate pet. The breed can also be independent and headstrong, which translates into too much canine intelligence for the inexperienced dog owner. Coat care for show-bred Springers is extensive, so owners of this type must enjoy grooming or be committed to taking their canine pal to a dog salon on a regular basis.

Springers require a good deal of early socialization to reach their full potential. Puppy classes and exposure to all types of environments when young is very important.

Training

English Springers are probably one of the easiest spaniel breeds to train. They are intelligent, truly want to please, and pick up commands quickly. One owner asked her Springer to sit at corners during a walk. Within a week, he was sitting automatically off-leash.

English Springers retain their youthful enthusiasm throughout their lives.

These spaniels master a house-breaking routine with relative ease. However, because they're clever dogs with a touch of the con artist, they learn early on what they can get away with. One three-month-old pup acted like she couldn't negotiate the stairs unassisted. She'd whimper and whine pitifully until the children in the family came to the rescue and carried her. This behavior went on for a while until "Mom" noticed the pup managed the stairs just fine when the children weren't home.

As a whole, the breed seems to enjoy learning, although they bore easily with too much repetition. Because they're soft-tempered, harsh methods are unnecessary and counterproductive. Although Springers can be headstrong, many may feel overwhelmed and even frightened of their trainers if physical corrections are employed. Motivational techniques, including verbal praise, toys, and food, reap far greater rewards.

English Springers like action and often learn moving commands, come, heel, and so on, more readily than sedentary ones. For example, a Springer may well fidget on a sit/stay when it should be still. Others struggle with the long sit and down commands, because they don't want to be parted from their owners at a distance. One fancier explained, after leaving her dog on a long down, he would scamper away and then lay down just two feet away from her.

It's hard to resist those spaniel eyes.

Sometimes Springer enthusiasm simply gets the best of these dogs. During a training session they may start jiggling, bouncing, and leaping all over the room. At moments like this it's often best to call it a day and begin anew another time.

It shouldn't come as a surprise that English Springers are true canine athletes. There's probably not a sport open to spaniels in which they cannot excel. Field-breds dominate field trials. Both types do well in areas where they must use their scenting abilities, whether it be in a tracking competition or on the job. At eight months old, Mindy was trained for drug detection work. She covers airports, and the coast of Maine with the Coast Guard. If there are drugs or drug-related items to be discovered, Mindy always finds them and is rewarded with a toss of her tennis ball. Bonnie, owned by the same family, was trained for bomb detection work. She has the acclaimed distinction of performing

Exercise and Grooming

English Springer Spaniels need a regular routine of exercise as an outlet for their energy. Although some are naturally more active than others, all will benefit from daily twenty-minute walks, games of fetch, and opportunities to run in a fenced yard or other safe enclosed space. For those who are unable to provide a fenced yard, more frequent daily walks are a good idea. Many Springers become restless and hyperactive in the home if their exercise needs are neglected. This is especially true of growing pups. When breeders receive frantic calls from their puppy buyers regarding ill behavior, increasing the level of exercise oftentimes cures the problem.

Adaptable dogs, Springers can adjust to urban life if their needs for exercise and personal attention are met. Mental stimulation is just as important as physical release. Springers benefit from the training and focus necessary to compete in the various canine sports.

Coat

With regard to grooming, pet show-breds should be combed and brushed at least twice a week to keep their silky coats lustrous and mat free. Special attention should be paid to the ears, armpits, and between the hind legs. Like all of the long-eared spaniels, Springers are prone to ear infections. About every three months the hair on the outer

Clearing a high jump.

searches for President Clinton, Vice President Al Gore, and former President Bush.

Because of their intelligence, honest desire to please, and aptitude for training, they are good choices for obedience competitors. However, more than one Springer owner has been exasperated in the ring. These dogs have an independent streak and though well versed in commands may on any given day refuse to execute an exercise. They understand full well what is expected of them but just don't feel like performing.

Their high energy and physical conformation makes them excellent agility dogs—a sport they love and master with minimal amounts of training. Like Cockers, they're consummate show dogs—a vision of canine beauty in the ring.

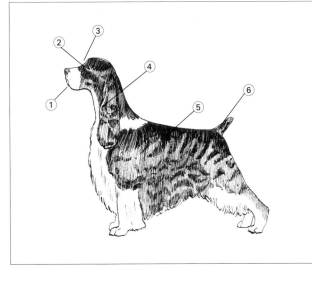
ear can be trimmed one third of the way down. Hair on the inner ear should also be kept short to help allow proper air circulation.

During routine trimming sessions, the head, muzzle, back of the neck, front of the neck (to the chest bone), tail, and paws can be trimmed with a number-ten blade. Hair between the paws should be trimmed with a number-15 blade or scissors. Feathering can be shaped with thinning shears. It's very important to keep foot hair short, as overgrowth can cause the foot to splay uncomfortably. Nail trimming and grooming feet will need to be done more frequently than the coat.

Some pet owners opt to trim the coat hair—a number-seven blade can be used for this area. However, the coat will not retain its silky texture if clippered. A bath every few months as needed should suffice.

Show dogs require more frequent baths and time-consuming grooming. They are brushed and combed several times during the week, clipped with blades that give a smoother appearance, and hand-stripped usually every two weeks.

The field-breds, with their shorter coats, are less maintenance. They may be brushed weekly, but can get by with longer intervals, keeping an eye out for mats behind the ears and in the armpits. Bathe as needed.

Breed-Specific Health Concerns

As previously mentioned, Springers have been known to suffer temperament problems with Canine Rage syndrome of particular concern. As with Cocker Spaniels, those potential dog owners who are interested in purchasing an English Springer must carefully research the breed before making a selection.

Springers have been known to suffer from retinal dysplasia. Occurring at birth, the retina is either curved, irregularly shaped, or possibly detached. Other potential health concerns are progressive retinal atrophy and hip dysplasia. To a lesser extent diabetes and epilepsy have also occurred.

Official Standard

General Appearance

The English Springer Spaniel is a medium-sized sporting dog, with a compact body and a docked tail. His coat is moderately long, with feathering on his legs, ears, chest and brisket. His pendulous ears, soft gentle expression, sturdy build and friendly wagging tail proclaim him unmistakably a member of the ancient family of Spaniels. He is above all a well-proportioned dog, free from exaggeration, nicely balanced in every part. His carriage is proud and upstanding, body deep, legs strong and muscular, with enough length to carry him with ease. Taken as a whole, the English Springer Spaniel suggests power, endurance and agility. He looks the part of a dog that can go, and keep going, under difficult hunting conditions. At his best, he is endowed with style, symmetry, balance and enthusiasm, and is every inch a sporting dog of distinct spaniel character, combining beauty and utility.

Size, Proportion, Substance

The Springer is built to cover rough ground with agility and reasonable speed. His structure suggests the capacity for endurance. He is to be kept to medium size. Ideal height at the shoulder for dogs is 20 inches; for bitches, it is 19 inches. Those more than one inch under or over the breed ideal are to be faulted. A 20 inch dog, well-proportioned and in good condition, will weigh approximately 50 pounds; a 19 inch bitch will weigh approximately 40 pounds. The length of the body (measured from point of shoulder to point of buttocks) is slightly greater than the height at the withers. The dog too long in body, especially when long in the loin, tires easily and lacks the compact outline characteristic of the breed. A dog too short in body for the length of his legs, a condition which destroys balance and restricts gait, is equally undesirable. A Springer with correct substance appears well-knit and sturdy with good bone, however, he is never coarse or ponderous.

Head

The head is impressive without being heavy. Its beauty lies in a combination of strength and refinement. It is important that its size and proportion be in balance with the rest of the dog. Viewed in profile, the head appears approximately the same length as the neck and blends with the body in substance. The stop, eyebrows and chiseling of the bony structure around the eye sockets contribute to the Springer's beautiful and characteristic expression, which is alert, kindly and trusting. The eyes, more than any other feature, are the essence of the Springer's appeal. Correct size, shape, placement and color influence expression and attractiveness. The eyes are of medium size and oval in shape, set rather well-apart and fairly deep in their sockets. The color of the iris harmonizes with the color of the coat, preferably dark hazel in the liver and white dogs and black or deep brown in the black and white dogs. Eyerims are fully pigmented and match the coat in color. Lids are tight with little or no haw showing. Eyes that are small, round or protruding, as well as eyes that are yellow or brassy in color, are highly undesirable. Ears are long and fairly wide, hanging close to the cheeks with no tendency to stand up or out. The ear leather is thin and approximately long enough to reach the tip of the nose. Correct ear set is on a level with the eye and not too far back on the skull. The skull is medium-length and fairly broad, flat on top and slightly rounded at the sides and back. The occiput bone is inconspicuous. As the skull rises from the foreface, it makes a stop, divided by a groove, or fluting, between the eyes. The groove disappears as it reaches the middle of the forehead. The amount of stop is moderate. It must not be a pronounced feature; rather it is a subtle rise where the muzzle joins the upper head. It is emphasized by the groove and by the position and shape of the eyebrows, which are well-developed. The muzzle is approximately the same length as the skull and one half the width of the skull. Viewed in profile, the toplines of the skull and muzzle lie in approximately parallel planes. The nasal bone is straight, with no inclination downward toward the tip of the nose, the latter giving an undesirable downfaced look. Neither is the nasal bone concave, resulting in a "dish-faced" profile; nor convex, giving the dog a Roman nose. The cheeks are flat, and the face is well-chiseled under the eyes. Jaws are of sufficient length to allow the dog to carry game easily: fairly square, lean and strong. The upper lips come down full and rather square to cover the line of the lower jaw, however, the lips are never pendulous or exaggerated. The nose is fully-pigmented, liver or black in color, depending on the color of the coat. The nostrils are well-opened and broad. Teeth are strong, clean, of good size and ideally meet in a close scissors bite. An even bite or one or two incisors slightly out of line are minor faults. Undershot, overshot and wry jaws are serious faults and are to be severely penalized.

Neck, Topline, Body

The neck is moderately long, muscular, clean and slightly arched at the crest. It blends gradually and smoothly into sloping shoulders. The portion of the topline from withers to tail is firm and slopes very gently. The body is short-coupled, strong and compact. The chest is deep, reaching the level of the elbows, with well-developed forechest; however, it is not so wide or round as to interfere with the action of the front legs. Ribs are fairly long, springing gradually to the middle of the body, then tapering as they approach the end of the ribbed section. The underline stays level with the elbows to a slight upcurve at the flank. The back is straight, strong and essentially level. Loins are strong, short and slightly arched. Hips are nicely-rounded, blending smoothly into the hind legs. The croup slopes gently to the set of the tail, and tail-set follows the natural line of the croup. The tail is carried horizontally or slightly elevated and displays a characteristic lively, merry action, particularly when the dog is on game. A clamped tail (indicating timidity or undependable temperament) is to be faulted, as is a tail carried at a right angle to the backline in Terrier fashion.

Forequarters

Efficient movement in front calls for proper forequarter assembly. The shoulder blades are flat and fairly close together at the tips, molding smoothly into the contour of the body. Ideally, when measured from the top of the withers to the point of the shoulder to the elbow, the shoulder blade and upper arm are of apparent equal length, forming an angle of nearly 90 degrees; this sets the front legs well under the body and places the elbows directly beneath the tips of the shoulder blades. Elbows lie close to the body. Forelegs are straight with the same degree of size continuing to the foot. Bone is strong, slightly flattened, not too round or too heavy. Pasterns are short, strong and slightly sloping, with no suggestion of weakness. Dewclaws are usually removed. Feet are round or slightly oval. They are compact and well-arched, of medium size with thick pads, and well-feathered between the toes.

Hindquarters

The Springer should be worked and shown in hard, muscular condition with well-developed hips and thighs. His whole rear assembly suggests strength and driving power. Thighs are broad and muscular. Stifle joints are strong. For functional efficiency, the angulation of the hindquarter is never greater than that of the forequarter, and not appreciably less. The hock joints are somewhat rounded, not small and sharp in contour. Rear pasterns are short (about $\frac{1}{3}$ the distance from the hip joint to the foot) and strong, with good bone. When viewed from behind, the rear pasterns are parallel. Dewclaws are usually removed. The feet are the same as in front, except that they are smaller and often more compact.

Coat

The Springer has an outer coat and an undercoat. On the body, the outer coat is of medium length, flat or wavy, and is easily distinguishable from the undercoat, which is short, soft and dense. The quantity of undercoat is affected by climate and season. When in combination, outer coat and undercoat serve to make the dog substantially waterproof, weatherproof and thornproof. On ears, chest, legs and belly the Springer is nicely furnished with a fringe of feathering of moderate length and heaviness. On the head, front of the forelegs, and below the hock joints on the front of the hind legs, the hair is short and fine. The coat has the clean, glossy, "live" appearance indicative of good health. It is legitimate to trim about the head, ears, neck and feet, to remove dead undercoat, and to thin and shorten excess feathering as required to enhance a smart, functional appearance. The tail may be trimmed, or well fringed with wavy feathering. Above all, the appearance should be natural. Overtrimming, especially the body coat, or any chopped, barbered or artificial effect is to be penalized in the show ring, as is excessive feathering that destroys the clean outline desirable in a sporting dog. Correct quality and condition of coat is to take precedence over quantity of coat.

Color

All the following combinations of colors and markings are equally acceptable:

1. Black or liver with white markings or predominantly white with black or liver markings;

2. Blue or liver roan;

3. Tricolor: black and white or liver and white with tan markings, usually found on eyebrows, cheeks, inside of ears and under the tail.

Any white portion of the coat may be flecked with ticking. Off colors such as lemon, red or orange are not to place.

Gait

The final test of the Springer's conformation and soundness is proper movement. Balance is a prerequisite to good movement. The front and rear assemblies must be equivalent in angulation and muscular development for the gait to be smooth and effortless. Shoulders which are well laid-back to permit a long stride are just as essential as the excellent rear quarters that provide driving power. Seen from the side, the Springer exhibits a long, ground-covering stride and carries a firm back, with no tendency to dip, roach or roll from side to side. From the front, the legs swing forward in a free and easy manner. Elbows have free action from the shoulders, and the legs show no tendency to cross or interfere. From behind, the rear legs reach well under the body, following on a line with the forelegs. As speed increases, there is a natural tendency for the legs to converge toward a center line of travel. Movement faults include high-stepping, wasted motion; short, choppy stride; crabbing; and moving with the feet wide, the latter giving roll or swing to the body.

Temperament

The typical Springer is friendly, eager to please, quick to learn and willing to obey. Such traits are conducive to tractability, which is essential for appropriate handler control in the field. In the show ring, he should exhibit poise and attentiveness and permit himself to be examined by the judge without resentment or cringing. Aggression toward people and aggression toward other dogs is not in keeping with sporting dog character and purpose and is not acceptable. Excessive timidity, with due allowance for puppies and novice exhibits, is to be equally penalized.

Summary

In evaluating the English Springer Spaniel, the overall picture is a primary consideration. One should look for type, which includes general appearance and outline, and also for soundness, which includes movement and temperament. Inasmuch as the dog with a smooth easy gait must be reasonably sound and well-balanced, he is to be highly regarded, however, not to the extent of forgiving him for not looking like an English Springer Spaniel. An atypical dog, too short or long in leg length or foreign in head or expression, may move well, but he is not to be preferred over a good all-round specimen that has a minor fault in movement. It must be remembered that the English Springer Spaniel is first and foremost a sporting dog of the Spaniel family, and he must look, behave and move in character.

Approval Date: February 12, 1994
Effective Date: March 31, 1994
© 1999 by the American Kennel Club.
Courtesy of the English Springer
Spaniel Field Trial Association, Inc.

Chapter Nine

The Field Spaniel

History

Nose to the ground, Cady charges through the underbrush—a brown streak, focused and determined. Moments later she stops suddenly, sits, and barks. Deputy Harley Simons sweeps aside the leaves and branches beneath his dog and finds her quarry—a sawed-off shotgun. He tosses a yellow tennis ball to Cady, praising her lavishly. The forty-pound Field Spaniel prances happily around Simons, squeezing her treasured reward.

Simons, of Pemberton, New Jersey, is a volunteer deputy conservation officer with the New Jersey Division of Fish, Game, and Wildlife's Bureau of Law Enforcement. Taking advantage of the Field Spaniel's hunting heritage, he has trained Cady as a guns and ammunition dog. She has become known as the Division's "secret weapon."

The Field Spaniel is one of the rarest sporting spaniels. In 1998, only 153 Fields were registered with the American Kennel Club. That this wonderful dog exists at all is a tribute to a few dedicated breeders.

Origin of the Breed

The Field was originally developed in the late 1800s by those who wanted a large, all-black spaniel capable of working in the field as well as retrieving from land and water. In those early days, dogs from the same litter could easily be referred to as different breeds depending on their size. Small black spaniels were considered Cockers, and their larger siblings were thought of as Fields.

Hunters didn't care what their dogs were called as long as they performed. However, when showing became popular, exhibitors needed to classify breeds and develop standards by which to compete.

In a short time the black Field Spaniel became a popular show dog. Too much so.

Dog show judges seemed to prize those dogs who were long and low to the ground. In an effort to meet this criterion, breeders got carried away and many unattractive, distorted-looking Fields emerged. As a result, the Field's popularity declined almost as quickly as its star had risen. The breed, which had been listed with the

Fields have been known to dive underwater to retrieve.

The Breed Today

Breed Description

Field Spaniels today are longer and lower to the ground than English Springer Spaniels, but in appealing proportions. Also heavier boned than Springers with larger feet, Fields stand roughly 18 inches (47 cm) high and weigh between 40 and 55 pounds (18–24.7 kg). Their coats can be black, liver (ranging from a light golden liver to dark chocolate), roan, or any of these colors with tan points. White markings on the solid colored dogs' throats and chests are also allowed.

The Field's elegant head, perhaps its finest feature, resembles the well-chiseled Irish Setter with long ears and muzzle. Their soft, silky coats are also setterlike and should be flat or slightly wavy, but never curly. Their expressive eyes range from dark hazel to dark brown. Like most of the sporting spaniels, tails are docked shortly after birth.

The Hunting Instinct

Although no longer bred specifically for hunting, Fields are very birdie and retain their hunting abilities. Apparently, the breed never achieved enough popularity to ruin their natural instincts. (When breeders strive for beauty in the show ring, no longer hunting their dogs generation after generation, working abilities can diminish.) They have excellent noses, work slowly, and are very thorough about every square foot they cover.

American Spaniel Club in the 1880s and later registered with the American Kennel Club (AKC) in 1894, nearly reached extinction by the early 1920s in the United States. Numbers dwindled in England as well.

Then in the late 1950s, serious breeders decided to bring the Field back. By crossing the few remaining Fieldies with English Springer Spaniels, they were able to create a breed that not only was more attractive than the low-slung dogs of the past, but one with a docile, pleasing personality who could make any hunter proud in the field.

Eventually in 1968, Richard Squire of Ohio and Carl Tuttle in Virginia imported three Fields from England and resurrected the breed in the United States. A decade later the Field Spaniel Society of America was formed and recognized by the AKC as the parent club for the breed.

When in the field, these spaniels excel in the underbrush. Their coats were designed to go through thickets, and they are extremely determined hunters. Some dogs have been seen crawling under blackberry bushes.

A fondness for water coupled with their fierce determination make Fields good water dogs as well. If a wounded duck dives under water, a Field will dive right in after it. They refuse to give up and sometimes must be forced to call it a day and return to their owners.

Although he doesn't hunt per se, by training Cady as a firearms detection dog, Deputy Simons has certainly channeled her hunting ability in a unique way. He enjoys watching Cady cover a field and believes she'd make a great bird dog. Of course he's very proud of her accomplishments—certainly a tribute to the Field's intelligence and aptitude for training. Cady has also captured the hearts of Simons and his wife on the home front. A very sweet-natured dog, she's affectionately referred to as the "love bucket."

Personality

Field Spaniels display an incredible zest for life. They are energetic, fun-loving, and mischievous, yet sweet and gentle. Less hyperactive than some of their spaniel cousins, Fields are best known for their laid-back attitude. Nothing much ruffles these docile dogs—they go with the flow and are very in tune to their owners' moods. If you want to putter in the garden, they'll oversee your efforts. Feel like jogging? They'll happily run by your side. If you need to wind down and read a book, they'll lie quietly at your feet.

Temperament

New owners may wonder when this easy-going temperament will show itself, as puppies can be inexhaustibly active. As a pup, my own dog, Smokey, jumped on counter tops, walked across radiators, and literally tried to climb trees. I thought he might be crazy and wasn't sure I'd survive his adolescence. Then at about nine months he began to mellow and eventually matured into a true gentleman, which is not unusual. These spaniels tend to mature very slowly and don't really reach adulthood until three or more years of age.

The original black Field Spaniel coat is still popular today.

The Field Spaniel's finely chiseled profile resembles the Irish Setter.

Fields are also less needy than some of the other breeds. They have the typical spaniel temperament of wanting to be with you—but don't have to lie in your lap. They're happy just to be in the same room.

Intelligent dogs, Fields have a reputation for figuring things out on their own. It's okay if their person doesn't want to participate in the activity of the moment; they will go merrily on their way devising their own games. Solo activities can include running laps around the yard, surveying the property, or simply playing with their toys.

Some Field owners claim their dogs are very adept at using their front paws like hands. One figured out how to turn the bathtub on by himself. Others have been known to open crate doors and cupboards.

The Great Outdoors

Adaptable dogs, Fields can adjust to life in a kennel if given plenty of attention. They also appreciate the comforts of the living room couch, a soft pillow, and a warm fire. However, they're probably happiest outdoors. Smokey bursts out the back door into his fenced-in yard with the same amount of gusto whether it's the first romp of the day or the tenth. Pet sitters are amazed by his enthusiasm.

Once outside, Fields love to sunbathe. If there's only one patch of sun in the yard, they will find it and lie there. If the chaise lounge happens to be in that spot, so much the better. Because of this obsession for the sun, some breeders recommend keeping coat oil with sunscreen on Field Spaniels, making sure their noses are protected as well.

Breed Characteristics

Fields have a strong passion for carrying something around in their mouths. It can be a toy, a slipper, or even their own ear if nothing else is available.

Some Fields are true kleptomaniacs with a real sense of humor. Presenting an embarrassing personal item to a visitor seems to be a favorite pastime for more than one Fieldie. Hoarding is another. Staying at a motel en route to a dog show, one exhibitor was incredulous when her Fieldie unpacked the suitcase and put everything in her crate, including the towels, while her unsuspecting owner was in the shower!

Fields are wonderfully devoted canine companions. They love to hug and cuddle by draping their paws over their owners' shoulders. And they're exceptionally good with children when raised with them, seeming to have constantly wagging tails. However, like most dogs who have not been exposed to children, they may be wary of them. Because of their docile natures, Fields will not act aggressively if threatened by a child's quick movements or behaviors. Instead, they're more inclined to leave the room. Quite heavy and strong for their size, Fields may be a little too much dog for toddlers or frail senior citizens.

With regard to strangers, most Fields tend to be cautious or aloof. Some have been known to hide behind furniture if a stranger approaches. Therefore, it's not a good idea to rush Fields into becoming friendly before they are ready. They prefer to take their time in sizing up a new person and making the first overture. It's best not to push the situation. Fields cannot stand being ignored. Ignoring them will bring them around faster than bestowing unwelcome attention.

Not all Fields are aloof. Some are quite outgoing. And they are very sociable with their own kind, whether it be a group of Fields living together or a single pet dog meeting new friends at the dog park. They seem to enjoy the company of other species as well and have been known to live peaceably with cats, ducks, and parrots.

At a pet show, one Field who lives with another dog and three birds, happily mingled with dogs, cats, rabbits, ferrets, and guinea pigs. Even when he suddenly came upon a hamster in a tiny harness and leash he simply sniffed the little guy, wagged his tail, and moved on.

Fields are generally quiet dogs around the house. Because of the breed's benign nature, they're not effective guard dogs. Several owners say, partly in jest, that their dogs would probably escort a robber around their homes making sure the thief found all the best stuff just because he seemed to be a "good guy."

And yet, because Fields have a very big, deep bark, and willingly sound off when strangers are on their property, they appear a lot more threatening than they actually are. Intruders would surely think twice before trying to enter a home

The Field's fondness for water lures this one in for a dip in the pool.

Enjoying the comforts of home, this Fieldie patiently waits for Santa.

inhabited by a Field, and so the breed does offer some "watch dog" protection.

Despite all of their wonderful traits, Fields do have some negative attributes, some of which were aptly described in an *AKC Gazette* article written by Winifred McCann, former-President of the Field Spaniel Society of America. "The Field is not the dog for those with 'House Beautiful' aspirations. Though seasonal shedding is only moderate, the large, heavily webbed feet eloquently testify to the breed's fondness for water; the Field is notorious for his drinking habits, which leave the floor around his bowl swamped, while long, wet ears create sluglike trails across a polished floor." Individual dogs may go one step further and lovingly place their heads on their owners' laps, completely soaking their apparel.

Many Fields snore, some, so much so, their owners have taken them to the vet fearing something might be wrong. They are also avid diggers and can be destructive when bored and if not given a job to perform.

True family dogs, Fields do not like feeling left out. A single pet may well howl—a long, low, pitiful wail if unhappy. Small packs sometimes feel a need for choir practice and will sound off like a chorus of hounds. They have a wide vocal range and some even yodel.

Fields don't like to share the attention of their owners with other dogs and have a habit of elbowing each other out of the way. They're also possessive of their belongings and have an "it's mine" attitude about their favorite toys. Interestingly, a toy becomes their "favorite" if another dog wants it.

For true Field enthusiasts these personality quirks are accepted or overlooked, because the breed's many fine qualities surely outweigh their drawbacks. I can attest that McCann's comments about the Field not being a dog for those with "House Beautiful" aspirations are quite accurate. Homes inhabited by Fieldies never stay clean for long. But somehow their sunny spirits make it all worthwhile.

Training

Most Field owners find housebreaking their dogs is a relatively easy task. Advanced formal training can be a little more difficult. On the one hand, they are a smart breed.

Obedience competitors have described their intelligence as similar to a Border Collie due to their rate of learning. Yet, while bright and generally willing to please, a Field can also be willful and stubborn, which is where the challenge lies.

Training Methods

A soft (sensitive) dog, a Field will only respond to behaviorally sound and positive training methods. Force training is a futile endeavor with this breed. Although they can take a strong correction physically, mentally they shut down. These dogs get insulted easily and aren't quick to forgive. If upset during training, it takes a long time to get them back. But, once they know what is expected of them, they usually do their job with enthusiasm and determination.

The general consensus among Field fanciers regarding training is to always make training sessions an upbeat and enjoyable experience for the dog. In other words, it's fairly easy if they think it's fun.

Speaking of fun, Fields are very athletic and excel at a myriad of dog sports. They're a nice breed for those owners who want to handle their own dogs in the show ring. They learn the routine quickly and are relatively simple to groom.

Due to lack of numbers, however, it is sometimes difficult to finish a Field's Championship. Those who have aspirations of multiple group placements and a number one sporting dog would be wise to select a more popular breed.

With proper training, Fields can excel in the obedience ring. They also do well in agility due to their balance, athleticism, and speed. And because of their excellent noses, tracking is another sport Fields master with ease.

In addition to sports, several Field Spaniel owners have taken advantage of the breed's docile disposition by becoming involved in pet therapy. Many feel they're ideal for this type of work. Daphne, who was the first Field certified as a Therapy Dog, seemed to understand a patient's physical limitations. She never placed her paws on a burn victim's legs, and she was very tolerant. One time an elderly woman pulled her by the ear; she reacted by placing her head in the woman's lap. Another Field, Geffrey, especially liked visiting senior citizens. He was

Preparing for the show ring.

very calm and gentle and would curl right up next to someone who was bedridden.

Exercise and Grooming

Despite their strong hunting instincts and love of the outdoors, Fields only require moderate amounts of exercise, but enjoy as much as they can get and at times seem tireless. Exercise can take the form of daily walks, ball chasing, or free play by themselves. They don't need a huge amount of space to run like some of the other sporting breeds do. Those fortunate enough to have two Fields report they get plenty of exercise frolicking between themselves.

Coat

The amount of grooming Fields require depends on their coats. Liver-colored dogs are more work,

Retrieving a dumbbell.

as they develop what is affectionately referred to as the "liver fuzzies," a thick furry coat that left ungroomed gives the dog a very bear-like appearance.

Generally, Fields are supposed to sport a natural look. Primarily the head, throat, and feet are the areas that require trimming. The coat should be brushed two to three times a week, and a bath given every few months as needed. Trimming can be done every six to eight weeks; however, this frequency isn't essential as it is with some of the heavier coated spaniels.

Special attention must be paid to Field paws; if left to grow naturally, it will look like they're wearing bedroom slippers and debris can get caught between their paw pads.

Electric clippers should never be used on the body of show dogs. This area should be stripped by hand or with a stripping knife if necessary. Pet owners who want to cheat in this regard, and give their dogs a neater appearance, can use a clipper with a number-seven blade or a 7½ skip tooth blade on the dog's body.

Breed-Specific Health Concerns

Generally, Field Spaniels enjoy good health and live long, active lives, many well into their teens. However, there are some health concerns Field fanciers should be

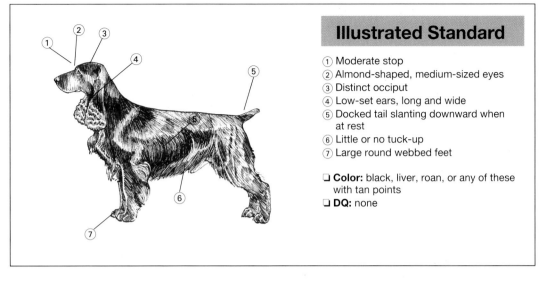

① Moderate stop
② Almond-shaped, medium-sized eyes
③ Distinct occiput
④ Low-set ears, long and wide
⑤ Docked tail slanting downward when at rest
⑥ Little or no tuck-up
⑦ Large round webbed feet

❏ **Color:** black, liver, roan, or any of these with tan points
❏ **DQ:** none

aware of, some relatively minor, others of a more serious nature.

Some young Fields, like other heavy-framed dogs, "go down at the pasterns" (a joint near the foot) during the teething stage of development. This means that the pasterns weaken and can be anything from a slight softening to a more obvious weakness. Puppies should be fed a good diet and only allowed limited, supervised exercise. Running up and down stairs or playing until they drop can be damaging to their proper development. Pastern problems generally resolve themselves as the dog ages. Pasterns that appear almost "broken" may be cause for greater concern and brought to the attention of the dog's breeder.

The Field's big webbed feet will attract mud, stones, and other sticky objects that can become ensnared in the hair, forming matted knots between the pads. So it's important to keep foot hair trimmed.

Some Field Spaniels are prone to ectropion and others suffer from thyroid disease. However, the major health issue in Fields is hip dysplasia. Fortunately, this problem has been kept to a minimum in the breed.

Official Standard

General Appearance

The Field Spaniel is a combination of beauty and utility. It is a well balanced, substantial hunter-companion of medium size, built for activity and endurance in heavy cover and water. It has a noble carriage; a proud but docile attitude; is sound and free moving. Symmetry, gait, attitude and purpose are more important than any one part.

Size, Proportion, Substance

Balance between these three components is essential.

Size: Ideal height for mature adults at the withers is 18 inches for dogs and 17 inches for bitches. A one inch deviation either way is acceptable.

Proportion: A well balanced dog, somewhat longer than tall. The ratio of length to height is approximately 7:6. (Length is measured on a level from the foremost point of the shoulder to the rearmost point of the buttocks.)

Substance: Solidly built, with moderate bone, and firm smooth muscles.

Head

Conveys the impression of high breeding, character and nobility, and must be in proportion to the size of the dog.

Expression: Grave, gentle, and intelligent.

Eyes: Almond in shape, open, and of medium size; set moderately wide and deep. Color: dark hazel to dark brown. The lids are tight and show no haw; rims comparable to nose in color.

Ears: Moderately long (reaching the end of the muzzle) and wide. Set on slightly below eye level: pendulous, hanging close to the head; rolled and well feathered. Leather is moderately heavy, supple, and rounded at the tip.

Skull: The crown is slightly wider at the back than at the brow and lightly arched laterally; sides and cheeks are straight and clean. The occiput is distinct and rounded. Brows are slightly raised. The stop is moderate, but well defined by the brows. The face is chiselled beneath the eyes.

Muzzle: Strong, long and lean, neither snipy nor squarely cut. The nasal bone is straight and slightly divergent from parallel, sloping downward toward the nose from the plane of the top skull. In profile, the lower plane curves gradually from the nose to throat. Jaws are level.

Nose: Large, fleshy and well developed with open nostrils. Set on as an extension of the muzzle. Color: solid: light to dark brown or black as befits the color of the coat.

Lips: Close fitting, clean, and sufficiently deep to cover the lower jaw without being pendulous.

Bite: Scissors or level, with complete dentition. Scissors preferred.

Neck, Topline, Body

Neck: Long, strong, muscular, slightly arched, clean, and well set into shoulders.

Topline: The neck slopes smoothly into the withers; the back is level, well muscled, firm and strong; the croup is short and gently rounded.

Body: The prosternum is prominent and well fleshed. The depth of chest is roughly equal to the length of the front leg from elbow to ground. The rib cage is long and extending into a short loin. Ribs are oval, well sprung, and curve gently into a firm loin.

Loin: Short, strong, and deep, with little or no tuck up.

Tail: Set on low, in line with the croup, just below the level of the back with a natural downward inclination. Docked tails preferred, natural tails are allowed. The tail whether docked or natural length should be in balance with the overall dog.

Forequarters

Shoulder blades are oblique and sloping. The upper arm is closed-set; elbows are directly below the withers, and turn neither in nor out. Bone is flat. Forelegs are straight and well boned to the feet. Pasterns are moderately sloping but strong. Dewclaws may be removed. Feet face forward and are large, rounded, and webbed, with strong, well arched relatively tight toes and thick pads.

Hindquarters

Strong and driving; stifles and hocks only moderately bent. Hocks well let down; pasterns relatively short, strong and parallel when viewed from the rear. Hips moderately broad and muscular; upper thigh broad and powerful; second thigh well muscled. Bone corresponds to that of the forelegs. No dewclaws.

Coat

Single; moderately long, flat or slightly wavy; silky and glossy; dense and water-repellent. Moderate setter-like feathering adorns the chest, underbody, backs of the legs,

buttocks, and may also be present on the second thigh and underside of the tail. Pasterns have clean outlines to the ground. There is short, soft hair between the toes. Over-abundance of coat, or cottony texture, impractical for field work should be penalized. Trimming is limited to that which enhances the natural appearance of the dog. Amount of coat or absence of coat should not be faulted as much as structural faults.

Color

Black, liver, golden liver, or shades thereof, in any intensity (dark or light); either self-colored or bi-colored. Bi-colored dogs must be roaned and/or ticked in white areas. Tan points are acceptable on the aforementioned colors and are the same as any normally tan pointed breed. White is allowed on the throat, chest, and/or brisket, and may be clear, ticked, or roaned on a self color dog.

Gait

The head is carried alertly, neither so high nor so low as to impede motion or stride. There is good forward reach that begins in the shoulder, coupled with strong drive from the rear, giving the characteristic effortless, long, low majestic stride. When viewed from front and/or rear elbows and hocks move parallel. The legs move straight, with slight convergence at increased speed. When moving, the tail is carried inclined slightly downward or level with the back, and with a wagging motion. Tail carried above the back is incorrect. Side movement is straight and clean, without energy wasting motions. Over-reaching and single tracking are incorrect. The Field Spaniel should be shown at its own natural speed in an endurance trot, preferably on a loose lead, in order to evaluate its movement.

Temperament

Unusually docile, sensitive, fun-loving, independent and intelligent, with a great affinity for human companionship. They may be somewhat reserved in initial meetings. Any display of shyness, fear, or aggression is to be severely penalized.

Approved: September 14, 1998
Effective: October 30, 1998
© 1998 by the American Kennel Club.
Courtesy of the Field Spaniel Society
of America

Chapter Ten

The Irish Water Spaniel

History

Three large, brown, curly-coated spaniels somersault onto their backs, wiggle, snort, and flail their legs with sheer delight. Rooming together en route to a dog show, the owners of these rambunctious Irish Water Spaniels howl with laughter, a reaction that only seems to encourage the dogs in their antics. It's not surprising. Irish Water Spaniels are considered the clowns of the spaniel world. Many fanciers claim their dogs love the sound of laughter and will go to great lengths to illicit this response.

Tallest of the sporting spaniels, with a tightly curled coat, unique top knot upon its head, and a long, smooth rat tail, the breed's very appearance may also contribute to the clownish reference.

Origin of the Breed

Of ancient lineage, there is archeological evidence of water spaniel type dogs in existence as far back as the 7th or 8th century A.D. Beyond that time, theories of origin vary and cannot be substantiated. Some believe early European Water Dogs, Poodles, and possibly even the Afghan Hound contributed to the development of the Irish Water Spaniel. Others feel the Irish Water Spaniel, Poodle, and Portuguese Water Dog share one common ancestor. It is known that two types of water spaniels eventually emerged in Ireland, one in the north country and one in the south. The northern variety was liver-colored with some white markings. It had short ears and a curly coat, with little feathering on the ears or legs. The southern dogs were solid liver and had long, well-feathered ears and a short full coat of tight curls. The modern day Irish Water Spaniel resembles the latter to a greater extent.

By the early 1800s, Justin M. McCarthy, an Irish sportsman and water spaniel enthusiast, bred Boatswain, the first true Irish Water Spaniel prototype. Although McCarthy liked to take credit for creating the Irish Water Spaniel, in all likelihood what he really did was stabilize the breed through selective breeding of the northern and southern varieties. Be that as it may, Boatswain, whelped (born) in 1834, is considered the original sire of the breed as we know it today. Now over a century later, his progeny look just like him.

Bred specifically to retrieve ducks and geese from rough cold waters, the Irish Water Spaniel quickly became popular with hunters of the day. News of these strong, courageous spaniels eventually reached our shores. By the late 1860s affluent Midwestern sportsmen began importing them. In no time their popularity spread to the east and west coasts. By 1875, the Irish Water Spaniel ranked as the third most popular sporting dog in this country.

However, these much-sought-after spaniels were dethroned in the 1950s when the far flashier and equally capable Labrador and Golden Retrievers emerged on the sport scene. These retrievers also had far-easier coats to maintain. Irish Waters never regained their popularity and are considered a rare

The Irish Water Spaniel is considered the clown of the spaniel world.

breed today with just over 100 dogs registered with the American Kennel Club each year.

The Breed Today

Classification

Because of their size, strength, and hunting heritage, the Irish Water Spaniel is the only spaniel classified as a retriever with the AKC. It is also the only spaniel allowed to compete in field trials and hunting tests designed for retrievers.

Despite their drop in popularity, Irish Waters are still fine hunting companions. They are bold and tireless workers. Not surprisingly, they are strong swimmers with a tremendous desire to retrieve. The breed profile produced by the Irish Water Spaniel Club of America eloquently describes the Irish Water Spaniel's water entry as "an explosion of eagerness, determination, and absolute lack of fear of the elements." Once these daring dogs hit the water, their webbed feet allow them to paddle with ease and their long tails act like rudders. Irish Waters will break through ice to reach a duck, retrieve it, and be ready and willing to do it again. And they are large enough to handle the Canadian goose as well as maneuver through thick muddy marshes. They are also capable of working upland game and think nothing of tearing through the toughest cover to find their quarry, or trail a running pheasant for as long as it takes to flush it into the air. Unfortunately, though, through no fault of their own, that thick curly coat can sidetrack them. On the one hand it protects the dog's skin from getting scratched by briars. But it also attracts burrs and other pesky hitchhikers like Velcro. And of course, a wet coat will surely slow the dog down. Some hunters solve the problem by giving their dogs a close trim for hunting season or spraying the coat with cooking oil before a day in the field to make removing burrs easier.

Breed Description

Irish Water Spaniels are eligible to participate in field trials, but because they are independent thinkers who balk at the repetitious drills required in competition, few actually do. Most are family pets and show dogs. A unique-looking breed, often confused with the Standard Poodle, the male Irish Water Spaniel stands between 22 and 24 inches (58–62 cm) at the shoulder and should weigh 55 to 65 pounds (24.7–29.2 kg). The female is slightly smaller, standing 21 to 23 inches (54–60 cm) and weighing 45 to 58 pounds (20.2–26.1 kg). The correct coat color is puce—a very dark liver with purplish cast. But it is not unusual to see various hues of liver. Their eyes are dark hazel. These dogs move with an unusual rollicking gate often described as "jaunty."

Irish Waters sport a double coat. The soft wooly undercoat provides warmth in cold weather and water.

The Irish Water Spaniel is very much at home by the water.

The tight, curly outer coat of crisp ringlets is slightly oily and water repellent. One fancier actually analyzed the Irish Water Spaniel coat and discovered it is comprised of hair and fur, with two types of strands, one coarse and wiry, the other wavy and curly. The Irish Water Spaniel has a smooth face and tail. Its head is crowned with a topknot of loose ringlets shadowing the eyes. The breed standard calls for a smooth spot on the inside of the front of the rear leg below the hock. Many dogs have an area of smoothness on their rears. A small area is acceptable, larger areas less so. Some dogs have no hair on their rears and partway down their back legs. Fanciers have a slang term for this condition that likens the look to a baboon's posterior. It is obviously not a desirable trait.

The Irish Water Spaniel's ringlets are very crisp and tight, whereas the Poodle's coat is looser and fluffier. The latter's tail is docked. It's face, body, and tail are trimmed in various styles. And of course, Poodles are bred in a variety of coat colors.

For some, the Irish Water Spaniel's unique appearance may be considered unappealing. But as in all things, beauty is truly in the eyes of the beholder. As one Irish Water Spaniel devotee so aptly put it, "They have won me over completely. Once I see that topknot and rat tail . . . I'm a gonner."

A unique-looking spaniel, the Irish Water Spaniel is often confused with the Standard Poodle.

Personality

The Irish Water Spaniel's personality compliments its clownish appearance. These dogs are happy, frolicking, playful, and at times downright goofy. They mature slowly—puppyhood can last for at least two years, their mischievous streak a lifetime.

Temperament

Unlike some of the other spaniels who attach themselves to one person, Irish Water Spaniels tend to devote themselves to the entire family. Their goal in life seems to be to please those they love and to make their people laugh through a variety of clever pranks.

One four-and-a-half-year-old female, Baily, enjoys sneaking socks out of her owner's drawer and carrying them around the house. Some days she swipes several different pairs without being noticed until bedtime. Then she lays on the bed and appears delighted to have discovered a sock hidden there. After it is taken away, suddenly another one shows up.

Baily wags her tail furiously throughout her performance but won't pull a sock out if her owners are looking. If they turn away, though, another one miraculously appears. After all the socks she's been hoarding throughout the day turn up, she somersaults onto her back, rolling, snorting, and kicking her feet wildly in the air.

Stealing clothes from the laundry is another favorite pastime for these

Irish Waters enjoy playing tricks on their owners.

mischievous water spaniels. One morning, Duffy, an obedience dog, snatched a pair of undergarments and pranced around with them in his mouth. By the time his owner walked out of the laundry room to take them away, Duffy had pulled the pants up over his front legs and seemed rather pleased to be wearing them. Quite a silly sight to be sure!

Not only do Irish Waters enjoy playing tricks on their owners they also have a dramatic flair. Baily has learned to stay on her property with the aid of an underground electric fence. With such a device, the dog wears a battery-operated collar. If it crosses over the line it receives a mild shock. Baily had gone almost two years without needing the collar but had started to step beyond the borders of her property. So her owner put the collar back on. Whenever she came within ten feet of the line, Baily would roll her eyes, drool, whimper, and fall to her side as if she was being beaten. Knowing she loves to dramatize and at that distance could only hear the warning buzzer, her owner wasn't too concerned. About two weeks later, however, Baily's mistress inadvertently crossed the electronic fence line herself carrying the collar. To her surprise, she didn't feel a shock. Upon investigation, she discovered there were no batteries in the collar. So Baily had repeatedly gone through her routine wearing an inactive collar. A good joke that one!!

Breed Characteristics

Obviously Irish Water Spaniels are an intelligent breed. They learn quickly, both positive and negative lessons. Owners must take charge early on or their dogs will gladly assume the role of pack leader. For this reason, they are probably not a good choice for first-time or too-lenient dog owners.

Because these dogs were bred to retrieve in rough, cold water, they are strong, energetic dogs with a great desire to work. Their energy and drive must be properly channelled with regular exercise, obedience training, field work, and/or other canine sport-

Irish Water Spaniels are a good breed for active families with older children.

ing activities. A nightly walk around the block will not suffice and can lead to having a frustrated dog with behavior problems.

They are a good breed for active families, especially those with older growing children who like to hike, camp, etc., and want a dog to be part of their lifestyle. Children must be respectful of their family pet as these dogs do not like chaos. They should also learn to talk to their dogs in a firm tone. Irish Water Spaniels like to run off with kids' toys, so the command "drop it" is especially important to master.

Irish Waters love to play all kinds of games and particularly enjoy swimming. They are probably too large and energetic for toddlers (unintentionally toppling a small one), busy parents who don't have time to meet their physical and psychological needs, and the elderly. Because these spaniels are such intelligent dogs, they require as much mental stimulation as physical activity.

Like the other breeds, Irish Waters are very devoted to their owners. People outside the family unit are of less interest. They usually meet strangers with a certain amount of reserve and suspicion. Because they are so rare, I was delighted to run into one waiting with his owner at a car wash. My enthusiasm about the encounter was not reciprocated. While by no way threatening, the dog stood his ground, looked me over with his hazel eyes, and gave an overall impression of "I really couldn't care less about you."

These dogs like to approach those they don't know on their own terms. They can be leery of unfamiliar children and do not like having little ones crawling all over them. Most will hide if overzealous behavior occurs.

Some Irish Water Spaniels are not particularly fond of other dogs either. In fact, males can be dog aggressive especially toward other Irish Waters. Fights are sure to break out if several males are housed together—a situation that is best to avoid. Interaction with other animals should be supervised.

Because of their devotion to their people, suspicion of strangers, and large size, Irish Water Spaniels make excellent watchdogs. Although unlikely to bite, a threatening Irish Water Spaniel is sure to deter a would-be robber. Though they will bark an alarm when necessary, they are generally quiet around the house.

Although individuals within the breed share common traits like high energy and retrieving instinct, it is actually difficult to make sweeping generalizations about these spaniels. Temperaments vary greatly even among littermates. Whereas one can be shy around strangers for example, another may be quite outgoing. Individual dogs can also exhibit Jekyll-and-Hyde aspects to their personalities. They can be willful and defiant one minute and loving and cuddly the next. Certainly, there is never a dull moment for those who share their lives with Irish Waters.

Training

Training the Irish Water Spaniel can be a challenge. Despite the fact that they are extremely intelligent and have a strong desire to work, they're also slow to mature, frequently stubborn, sometimes willful, and very curious. Anything new or unusual in their environment needs to be checked out. And it needn't be anything particularly suspicious. A freshly sprouted batch of mushrooms on the front lawn caught one Irish Water's attention and needed to be investigated immediately. These dogs seem to be extremely "visually aware," especially of objects above their eye level that can cause a certain amount of apprehension. This intense curiosity often distracts them during formal training causing them to wander away from the work at hand.

Not surprisingly, Irish Water Spaniels love to swim.

The breed is also known for its "creative thinking." Although they want to please their people, Irish Water Spaniels frequently have their own take on how things should be done, often to the amusement of others.

One day, Tucker, an Irish Water Spaniel being trained in advanced obedience work, entered a trial. His owner was instructed to send her dog over the high jump to retrieve a dumbbell. As she did so a competitor in the adjacent ring had also just instructed her Golden Retriever to fetch. Tucker sailed over the ring barrier, snatched the dumbbell from the unsuspecting Golden's mouth, leaped back over the barrier, and gave it to his owner. The unexpected performance drew hysterical laughter from the crowd.

Training Methods

Because of their intelligence, Irish Water Spaniels are easily bored. They cannot tolerate repetitious drilling. And for that very reason may not be good dogs for sportsmen who want to participate in retriever field trials. They are better suited to hunt tests, as this sporting activity is less rigorous and demanding.

When they are in the mood to cooperate, Irish Water Spaniels are extremely focused. They learn and retain their lessons quickly. They also learn by observation, i.e.: how to open kitchen cabinets, laundry dryers, and so on. They're also very adept at stealing food off kitchen counters and must be taught early on that counter tops are off limits.

Bright, cocky, and sometimes domineering as they can be, Irish Water Spaniels are still spaniels at heart with sensitive natures. Harsh training methods are unnecessary and counterproductive. To their credit, these dogs are more forgiving of sharp corrections than some of the other breeds.

Because of their low registration numbers, most Irish Water Spaniels are owner-handled in the breed ring. Some of the dogs enjoy the fuss and attention, others do not like being touched by the judge and have been known to collapse to the ground in protest. It can be difficult to finish a championship in areas where few Irish Water Spaniels reside. Still, there have been some very impressive Irish Water Spaniel show dogs. In 1979, a representative of the breed took Best in Show at the prestigious Westminster Kennel Club Show in New York City. In 1990 and 1991, another Irish Water Spaniel won the Sporting Group again at Westminster.

Obedience and Agility Trials

Because of their intelligence and aptitude for training, Irish Waters can do well in obedience trials. However, because of their disdain for repetition and propensity for pranks, they place less consistently than some of the obedience star breeds. For example, it took one Irish Water Spaniel over forty tries to earn her Companion Dog Excellent title, even though she was quite familiar with the commands. Interestingly, the Irish Water Spaniel was the first sporting dog in the United States to earn an obedience title.

Because of their athleticism, willingness to work with people, and love of challenge, Irish Waters are excellent agility dogs. They're fast, good jumpers, and like working as a team. They also take to tracking with great zeal. Depending on the terrain, however, their coats may have to be trimmed to participate in this sport.

Exercise and Grooming

Irish Water Spaniels are extremely active puppies and continue to have high levels of energy throughout their lives. They often leap into the air for the sheer joy of it. Daily exercise in the form of long walks, Frisbee games, ball catching, and romps in secure areas are essential to meet their needs. This is not a breed that can miss a walk for a day or two and be expected to lay contentedly around the house. A frustrated and bored Irish Water Spaniel is trouble waiting to happen. Swimming, obedience, and agility training are wonderful outlets for this active spaniel.

Coat

Irish Water Spaniels also require a regular grooming routine to maintain a healthy and attractive coat. A good comb out once or twice a week is recommended to avoid matting. Scissoring to neaten the appearance should be done every six to eight weeks.

Irish Water Spaniels are extremely active puppies.

These dogs shed slightly throughout the year and drop coat (go through a period of heavier shedding) in the spring and fall. Their hair grows continually and stray hairs clump together in little "dust bunnies" when shed, which actually lends itself to quick clean up. Regular baths or swimming opportunities help maintain the correct, tightly curled ringlets.

Irish Water Spaniel owners must be committed to routine grooming or the coat can become severely matted, promoting skin disease. These spaniels have little dander, which makes them easily tolerated by dog lovers with allergies.

Breed-Specific Health Concerns

Irish Water Spaniels are hardy dogs. However, special attention should be paid to ear hygiene, especially if they swim frequently. Because of the Velcro-type coat, certain field conditions should be avoided by hunters, or as an alternative the coat closely trimmed.

The Irish Water Spaniel is generally a healthy breed. But as with all of its relatives, certain problems do occur. The most commonly seen are hip dysplasia, epilepsy, and hypothyroidism. Nail bed disease, skin conditions, and entropian also exist. According to the breed profile produced by the parent club, veterinarians should be made aware there have been reports of breed sensitivity to ivermectin (a worming medi-cine), sulfa drugs (antimicrobial), and some types of anesthesia.

Official Standard

General Appearance

The Irish Water Spaniel presents a picture of a smart, upstanding strongly built sporting dog. Great intelligence is combined with rugged endurance and a bold, dashing eagerness of temperament. Distinguishing characteristics are a topknot of long, loose curls, a body covered with a dense, crisply curled liver colored coat, contrasted by a smooth face and a smooth "rat" tail.

Size, Proportion, Substance

Strongly built and well boned, the Irish Water Spaniel is a dog of medium length, slightly rectangular in

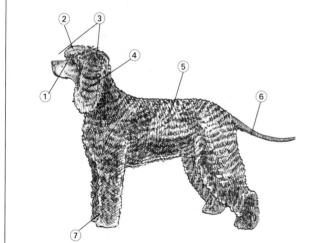

Illustrated Standard

① Medium-sized almond-shaped eyes, hazel in color
② Topknot consisting of long loose curls
③ Prominent occiput and gradual stop
④ Low-set, long ears
⑤ Topline level or slightly higher in rear
⑥ "Rat" tail, thick and covered with curls at base only, tapering to a fine point at end, carried nearly level with back
⑦ Large feet

❏ **Color:** solid liver
❏ **DQ:** none

appearance. He is well balanced and shows no legginess or coarseness. Dogs 22 to 24 inches, bitches 21 to 23 inches, measured at the highest point of the shoulder. Dogs 55 to 65 pounds, bitches 45 to 58 pounds.

Head

The head is cleanly chiseled, not cheeky, and should not present a short, wedge shaped appearance. The skull is rather large and high in the dome, with a prominent occiput and a gradual stop. The muzzle is square and rather long, with a deep mouth opening and lips fine in texture. The nose large and liver in color. Teeth strong and regular with a scissors or level bite. The hair on the face is short and smooth, except for a beard which grows in a narrow line at the back of the jaw.

Topknot: A characteristic of the breed, consists of long, loose curls growing down into a well-defined peak between the eyes and falling like a shawl over the tops of the ears and occiput. Trimming of this breed characteristic in an exaggerated manner is highly objectionable.

Eyes: Medium in size, slightly almond shaped with tight eyelids. Eyes are hazel in color, preferably of a dark shade. The expression is keenly alert, intelligent, direct and quizzical.

Ears: Long, lobular, set low, with leathers reaching about to the end of the nose when extended forward, and abundantly covered with long curls, extending two or more inches below the tips of the leathers.

Neck, Topline, Body

Neck: The neck is long, arching, strong and muscular; smoothly set into cleanly sloping shoulders.

Topline: Strong and level, or slightly higher in the rear; never descending, or showing sag or roach.

Body: The body is of medium length, slightly rectangular. Chest deep, with brisket extending to the elbows. Ribs well sprung and carried well back. Immediately behind the shoulders ribs are flattened enough to allow free movement of the forelegs, becoming rounder behind. Loin short, wide and muscular. The body should not present a tucked-up appearance.

Forequarters

The entire front gives the impression of strength without heaviness. Shoulders are sloping and clean. Forelegs well boned, muscular, medium in length; with sufficient length of upper arm to ensure efficient reach. Elbows close set. Forefeet are large, thick and somewhat spreading; well clothed with hair both over and between the toes.

Hindquarters

Sound hindquarters are of great importance to provide swimming power and drive. They should be as high or slightly higher than the shoulders, powerful and muscular, with well developed upper and second thighs. Hips wide, stifles moderately bent, hocks low set and moderately bent. Rear angulation is moderate, and balance of front and rear angulation is of paramount importance. Rear feet are large, thick and somewhat spreading; well clothed with hair. Tail should be set on low enough to give a rather rounded appearance to the hindquarters and should be carried nearly level with the back.

Tail

The so-called "rat tail" is a striking characteristic of the breed. At the root it is thick and covered for two or three inches with short curls. It tapers to a fine point at the end; and from the root curls is covered with short, smooth hair so as to look as if it had been clipped. The tail should not be long enough to reach the hock joint.

Coat

Proper double coat is of vital importance to protect the dog while working. The neck, back, sides, and rear are densely covered with tight, crisp ringlets, with the hair longer underneath the ribs. Forelegs are well covered with abundant curls or waves. The hind legs should also be abundantly covered by hair falling in curls or waves, except that the hair should be short and smooth on the front of the legs below the hocks. The hair on the throat is very short and smooth, forming a V-shaped patch. All curled areas should be clearly defined by curls of sufficient length to form a sharp contrast with the smooth coat on face, throat, tail, and rear legs below the hocks. Fore and hind feet should be well clothed with hair both over and between the toes. Dogs may be shown in natural coat or trimmed. However, no dog should be groomed or trimmed so excessively as to obscure the curl or texture of the coat.

Color

Solid liver. With the exception of graying due to age, white hair or markings objectionable.

Gait

The Irish Water Spaniel moves with a smooth, free, ground covering action that, when viewed from the side, exhibits balanced reach and drive. True and precise coming and going. When walking or standing, the legs are perpendicular to the ground, toeing neither in nor out.

Temperament

Very alert and inquisitive, the Irish Water Spaniel is often reserved with strangers. However, aggressive behavior or excessive shyness should be penalized. A stable temperament is essential in a hunting dog.

Faults

The foregoing description is that of the ideal Irish Water Spaniel in hard working condition. Any deviation from the above described dog must be penalized to the extent of the deviation, keeping in mind the importance of the various features toward the basic original purpose of the breed.

Approved June 12, 1990
Effective August 1, 1990
© 1997 by the American Kennel Club.
Courtesy of the Irish Water Spaniel
Club of America

Chapter Eleven

The Sussex Spaniel

History

The gentleman farmer strolls across his grounds while his two Sussex Spaniels amble along beside him. Tails in constant motion, their golden liver coats shimmer in the summer sun. One catches a scent and picks up speed. Soon the two take to the woods to investigate. The scene is reminiscent of a bygone era, a time when Sussex Spaniels were owned by the British gentry.

The rarest of the sporting spaniels, in fact one of the rarest dog breeds recognized by the AKC (136 out of 146), the Sussex was originally bred in the southeastern regions of England known as the county of Sussex. Landowners of the time needed a strong, determined gun dog able to penetrate the abundant thick deep cover found on their estates. The Sussex Spaniel with its short legs and long muscular body was well suited for the job.

Origin of the Breed

Though no one knows for sure, it is believed a hound and the Tweed Water Spaniel contributed to the development of the Sussex. One particular fancier, a Mr. Fuller, is considered the father of the breed. In 1795, he established Rosehill Park Kennel in Sussex, and along with his kennel master, Albert Relf, purified the unique golden liver color. When Fuller passed away in 1847, Relf kept up the breeding program for the next forty years. Always few in number, the Sussex may have become extinct had Relf not been dedicated to perpetuating the breed.

Over the years interest in preserving the Sussex Spaniel ebbed and flowed. When World War II broke out, dog fanciers were forced to curtail their breeding programs. The Sussex once again faced extinction. Truly alarmed, Joyce Freer of Four-clovers Kennel was determined to save her beloved spaniels. Sometimes going without food herself, she managed to feed and care for her eight dogs. She was even able to breed several litters. Her dogs survived the war, and Mrs. Freer had literally saved the Sussex Spaniel.

American fanciers began importing the Sussex in the late 1800s. The breed was the fifth to be recognized

The Sussex Spaniel is one of the rarest dog breeds recognized by the AKC.

as they soon realize birds are often hidden within them.

Although Sussex Spaniels have keen noses and excellent tracking abilities, easily marking and flushing their quarry, most are not inclined to retrieve. Some like to "give tongue" (bark or make some other sound) when they are about to flush. What they lack in speed they compensate for with stamina. Sussex Spaniels can and happily will hunt all day long.

Breed Description

According to the breed standard these talented gun dogs should stand between 13 and 15 inches (34–39 cm) and weigh between 35 and 45 pounds (15.7–20.2 kg). Long and low, the breed is described as having a massive build. They have broad heads, carried just slightly above the level of the back, with a heavy brow. Sporting a coarse outer coat and wooly undercoat, their tails are docked to a length of five to seven inches.

by the AKC. For many years interest and commitment to these spaniels wavered. Their survival was again threatened. Finally in the early 1970s, they found staunch supporters in George and Marcia Deugan. To this day the Deugans champion their rare breed under their Ziyadah Kennnel banner. In 1981, the Sussex Spaniel Club of America was formed.

The Breed Today

Despite their rocky history, Sussex Spaniels remain fine gun dogs. They hunt at a slower, more methodical pace than some of their leggier cousins. Working well naturally within gun range, they require little formal training. They're especially adept at hunting in thick and thorny territory just as their ancestors before them. In fact, they seem to gravitate toward these more difficult and dense areas

Personality

Regardless of appearances to the contrary, Sussex Spaniels are not larger, cuddlier Cockers. These dogs have some very distinct personality traits and behaviors. Similar to the other spaniel breeds, Sussex Spaniels are very loyal to their people. Although they may not cling to their owners as closely as some of the others, they do keep an eye on things. They're good family dogs, often attaching themselves to one particular person. They love to be the center of attention and enjoy a good snuggle. In fact, the breed has a habit of sitting up on its haunches in a great gopher imitation. Some do this outdoors, alone in a chair, or propped on their owners' laps. One female, Diana, has perfected the technique. She sits ramrod straight and leans back against her mistress, exposing her belly for a tummy rub. If her owner stops petting, Diana swats her hand with a front paw to continue.

Temperament

Although Sussex Spaniels share a devotion to their people with their spaniel cousins, they are far more territorial and protective of their homes than many of the other breeds. Although not generally aggressive, if given sufficient provocation—say an intruder breaking into the house, the Sussex will bark menacingly and may well bite.

Sussex are generally reserved around strangers but usually become friendly when they realize properly invited guests should be welcomed. They tend to be more outgoing and accepting of strangers away from their homes and property.

These spaniels can be wonderful dogs with children if raised with them from puppyhood. They may be less tolerant of unfamiliar children running in and out of the house and causing a lot of commotion. It is not a breed that is likely to ignore perceived abuse, i.e., roughhousing or teasing from disrespectful children.

Sussex Spaniels also do not appreciate sharing their homes with other dogs. Most want to be Alpha and will fight to maintain their rank. They become especially jealous when other dogs vie for their owner's attention. Disputes can also erupt over ownership of toys. Generally, the Sussex prefers to be an "only dog." Interestingly, the breed is more accepting of fellow canines they meet away from home and do not have to live with.

The breed's hunting instinct may be too strong for them to reliably accept other pets such as cats, rabbits, and birds. Although certain individuals may get along well, early socialization around other species and lots of supervision is prudent.

A dog that thoroughly enjoys sleeping, Sussex Spaniels are couch potatoes a good deal of the time. Owners often find them splayed out on their backs, front legs flopping

The Sussex Spaniel remains a fine gun dog.

The Sussex Spaniel is known for its great gopher imitation.

Once on vacation touring an old village, she jumped into a horse trough leash and all.

The Sussex isn't too particularly concerned with cleanliness. In fact, slopping through a muddy marsh is just as much fun as a dip in the pool. Being covered in dirt is fine with them. This disinterest in cleanliness can affect housebreaking. Sussex Spaniels will use their crates as a bathroom, something most dogs loathe to do, if their owners are not diligent about getting them outside at frequent intervals. Many Sussex Spaniels also have a habit of drooling. This usually occurs when they get a whiff of dinner, after a drink of water, or on a hot summer day.

In addition to their brown coats tinged with golden yellow highlights, Sussex Spaniels have a unique rollicking gait, where their back legs move together in unison. Although they don't require as much exercise as many other sporting dogs, a good daily walk or romp in the yard will be appreciated and help keep the Sussex fit. However, they won't get hyperactive if regular exercise is neglected now and them. They're quite content to keep pace with their owners' routine and activity level.

These dogs are very curious by nature. Diana is mesmerized by anything that moves, be it bugs, leaves blowing in the wind, or beams of sunlight. She watches all of these intently, a trait shared with many of her relatives.

As a pup, Diana and her canine housemate were safely locked in the

from their sides, back legs extended. However, when they're awake they love to play and have fun just like all the other breeds.

Breed Characteristics

The slow methodical pace the Sussex Spaniels are known for in the field does not translate into their being slugs around the house. These dogs have plenty of energy and stamina to keep up with an active family. Some particularly like water. One female, Fergie, will dive into anything wet with an expression of sheer delight on her face. Her owners have a pond on their property and also provide her with a child's wading pool. But she also can't resist putting her paws in her water dish and trying to sit in it.

kitchen when their owners went out. Left to their own devices, the pups discovered a case of cola and proceeded to puncture the cans. When their owners returned, the two cohorts seemed to be having a wonderful time watching soda squirt everything in sight!

Obviously, Sussex Spaniels have a mischievous streak. They're merry dogs expressing their joy with constantly wagging tails. They often grin by pulling their lips up and exposing their teeth. The breed also has a distinctive "roo," a high pitched bay they use when feeling lonely or neglected. They also enjoy howling in harmony.

Although Sussex Spaniels are affectionate dogs, they are powerful animals with strong personalities. Slow to mature with a pension for doing things their own way, they would not make suitable pets for senior citizens or first-time dog owners. Those who understand canine behavior and can establish pack leadership early on may well appreciate the company of these charming yet challenging spaniels.

Training

Similar to the water spaniels, Sussex display interesting contradictions in their personalities. On the one hand, they are bold, protective dogs. But when it comes to training, they can be highly sensitive, reacting in pitiful protest if treated too harshly.

Appearances to the contrary, the Sussex Spaniel has plenty of energy and stamina.

These spaniels, though bright in their own right, are often slow to learn specific commands. Every routine must be broken down into small segments, each part mastered before the entire exercise is understood.

Training Methods

They definitely have a stubborn streak and some days are disinterested in—even resistant to—training. They can be manipulative and quite adept at getting away with being naughty. A Sussex owner must be firm with commands and follow through, keeping one step ahead of their dogs.

Interestingly, Sussex fanciers have witnessed a wide range in temperament and aptitude for training within the breed, which is curious since these dogs are so few in number and closely related.

These spaniels are curious by nature.

Whereas some breeds are highly motivated by food rewards, Sussex Spaniels are more apt to respond to praise and approval. Just as they are very in tune to their owner's whereabouts in the house, they will keep their attention on their person during training. This doesn't mean they will necessarily do what they've been told, only that they're listening.

Although Sussex Spaniels may be slow to master formal exercises, they're quick to learn commands they can use to their advantage. One clever female was taught to ring a bell when she needed to go into the yard to relieve herself. She soon understood the connection between the bell and being let outside. If she felt her owner was spending too much time on the phone, she'd promptly ring her bell, thereby ending the conversation.

Prospective spaniel owners who have hopes of doing well in obedience would probably be better off selecting one of the easier-to-train breeds. However, if their interests lie in tracking or hunt tests, the Sussex can be ideal. They love these sports and excel in both.

They can also do well in conformation. Judges tend to enjoy their jovial natures. However, it may be difficult to complete a championship because the breed is so rare.

Exercise and Grooming

Described as a "wash and wear" breed, Sussex Spaniels are generally easy to care for. They don't require as much exercise as many of their relatives and will not become hyperactive if athletic pursuits are sometimes neglected. However, a daily walk or romp is good for their physical and mental health.

Long-distance walkers may enjoy the company of the Sussex, who can easily keep up. One fancier, who regularly backpacks with several Sussex Spaniels, once scaled a 10,000-foot (2,960-m) mountain, covering thirty miles (48 km) in 13 hours with his dogs.

Coat

These spaniels should receive a good brushing once or twice a week. Because they tend to mat behind

The Sussex is an expert hunter in dense terrain.

their ears and in their "arm pits," regular brushing and removing mats as soon as they form is advised. Their nails and the hair between their paw pads should be trimmed every few weeks. Feathers should be neatened as needed.

Ears must be cleaned routinely to avoid infections. A bath every four to six weeks will keep a Sussex Spaniel looking its best and combat doggy odor.

Breed-Specific Health Concerns

Sussex Spaniels can have trouble breeding, conceiving, and whelping. However, the greatest concern in the breed is congenital heart problems. Pups with these defects can die at birth or within the first few years of life.

Other potential problems include: entropion, thyroid disease, and hip dysplasia. The breed also tends to get a buildup of excess tartar and can lose teeth as a result at a relatively early age of six or seven years.

Official Standard

General Appearance

The Sussex Spaniel was among the first ten breeds to be recognized and admitted to the Stud Book when the American Kennel Club was formed in 1884, but it has existed as a distinct breed for much longer. As its name implies, it derives its origin from the county of Sussex, England, and it was used there since the eighteenth century as a field dog. During the late 1800s the reputation of the Sussex Spaniel as an excellent hunting companion was well known among the estates surrounding Sussex County. Its short legs, massive build, long body, and habit of giving tongue when on scent made the breed ideally suited to penetrating the dense undergrowth and flushing game within range of the gun. Strength, maneuverability, and desire were essential for this purpose. Although it has never gained great popularity in numbers, the Sussex Spaniel continues today essentially unchanged in character and general appearance from those 19th-century sporting dogs. The Sussex Spaniel presents a long and low, rectangular and rather massive appearance coupled with free movements and nice tail action. The breed has a somber and serious expression. The rich golden liver color is unique to the breed.

A proud moment.

Size, Proportion, Substance

Size: The height of the Sussex Spaniel as measured at the withers ranges from 13 to 15 inches. Any deviation from these measurements is a minor fault. The weight of the Sussex Spaniel ranges between 35 and 45 pounds.

Proportion: The Sussex Spaniel presents a rectangular outline as the breed is longer in body than it is tall.

Substance: The Sussex Spaniel is muscular and rather massive.

Head

Correct head and expression are important features of the breed.

Eyes: The eyes are hazel in color, fairly large, soft and languishing, but do not show the haw overmuch.

Expression: The Sussex Spaniel has a somber and serious appearance, and its fairly heavy brows produce a frowning expression.

Ears: The ears are thick, fairly large, and lobe-shaped and are set moderately low, slightly above the outside corner of the eye.

Skull and Muzzle: The skull is moderately long and also wide with an indentation in the middle and with a full stop. The brows are fairly heavy, the occiput is full but not pointed, the whole giving an appearance of heaviness without dullness. The muzzle should be approximately three inches long, broad, and square in profile. The skull as measured from the stop to the occiput is longer than the muzzle. The nostrils are well-developed and liver colored. The lips are somewhat pendulous.

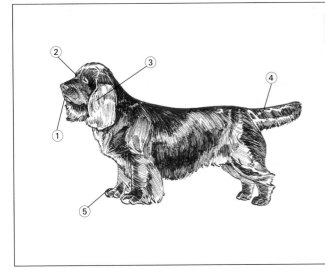

Illustrated Standard

1. Somewhat pendulous lips
2. Eyes soft and languishing, fairly large, hazel colored
3. Large, low-set ears
4. Tail docked from 5 to 7"
5. Large round feet, with long feathering

❏ **Color:** rich golden liver
❏ **DQ:** none

Bite: A scissors bite is preferred. Any deviation from a scissors bite is a minor fault.

Neck, Topline, Body

Neck: The neck is rather short, strong, and slightly arched, but does not carry the head much above the level of the back. There should not be much throatiness about the skin.

Topline and Body: The whole body is characterized as low and long with a level topline. The chest is round, especially behind the shoulders, and is deep and wide which gives a good girth. The back and loin are long and very muscular both in width and depth. For this development, the back ribs must be deep.

Tail: The tail is docked from 5 to 7 inches and set low. When gaiting the Sussex Spaniel exhibits nice tail action, but does not carry the tail above the level of the back.

Forequarters

The shoulders are well laid back and muscular. The upper arm should correspond in length and angle of return to the shoulder blade so that the legs are set well under the dog. The forelegs should be very short, strong, and heavily boned. They may show a slight bow. Both straight and slightly bowed constructions are proper and correct. The pasterns are very short and heavily boned. The feet are large and round with short hair between the toes.

Hindquarters

The hindquarters are full and well-rounded, strong, and heavily boned. They should be parallel with each other and also set wide apart—about as wide as the dog at the shoulders. The hind legs are short from the hock to the ground, heavily boned, and should seem neither shorter than the forelegs nor much bent at the hocks. The hindquarters must correspond in angulation to the forequarters. The hocks should turn neither in nor out. The rear feet are like the front feet.

Coat

The body coat is abundant, flat or slightly waved, with no tendency to curl. The legs are moderately well-feathered, but clean below the hocks. The ears are furnished with soft, wavy hair. The neck has a well-marked frill in the coat. The tail is thickly covered with moderately long feather. No trimming is acceptable except to shape foot feather, or to remove feather between the pads or between the hock and the feet. The feather between the toes must be left in sufficient length to cover the nails.

Color

Rich golden liver is the only acceptable color and is a certain sign of the purity of the breed. Dark liver or puce is a major fault. White on the chest is a minor fault. White on any other part of the body is a major fault.

Gait

The round, deep and wide chest of the Sussex Spaniel coupled with its short legs and long body produce a rolling gait. While its movement is deliberate, the Sussex Spaniel is in no sense clumsy. Gait is powerful and true with perfect coordination between the front and hind legs. The front legs do not paddle, wave, or overlap. The head is held low when gaiting. The breed should be shown on a loose lead so that its natural gait is evident.

Temperament

Despite its somber and serious expression, the breed is friendly and has a cheerful and tractable disposition.

Faults

The standard ranks features of the breed into three categories. The most important features of the breed are color and general appearance. The features of secondary importance are the head, ears, back and back ribs, legs, and feet. The features of lesser importance are the eyes, nose, neck, chest and shoulders, tail, and coat. Faults also fall into three categories. Major faults are color that is too light or too dark, white on any part of the body other than the chest, and a curled coat. Serious faults are a narrow head, weak muzzle, the presence of a topknot, and a general appearance that is sour and crouching. Minor faults are light eyes, white on chest, the deviation from proper height ranges, lightness of bone, shortness of body or a body that is flat-sided, and a bite other than scissors. There are no disqualifications in the Sussex Spaniel standard.

Approved April 7, 1992
Effective May 27, 1992
© 1997 by the American Kennel Club.
Courtesy of the Sussex Spaniel Club
of America

Chapter Twelve

The Welsh Springer Spaniel

History

Invariably his eyes sparkle as he speaks with unbridled enthusiasm, hands gesturing for emphasis, about a great day in the field. If you really listen, you will feel his excitement, understand his pride, and instinctively sense the intensity of the bond between a hunter and his dog.

Origin of the Breed

Though every dog owner surely feels the relationship with his canine companion is unique, and rightly so, the special communication between hunters and dogs has developed over centuries. Ironically, one of man's oldest hunting partners is relatively unknown here in the United States. The Welsh Springer Spaniel, a medium-sized dog with a distinctive red and white coat, has been in existence for quite some time. Although the actual date of origin cannot be traced, studies of old pictures and prints frequently depict a spaniel closely resembling the Welsh Springer. In all probability these dogs were the ancestors of the Welsh, as the red and white markings are one of the breed's distinguishing features. These Springers, often referred to as "starters" because of their natural ability to start (spring) game, have been known principally in Wales and the west of England for hundreds of years. According to The Welsh Springer Spaniel Club of America (WSSCA), founded in 1961, the Welsh Springer came into prominence about 1800 when the Williams family of Wales appeared with the breed at field trials and shows. At the same time, other lines were owned and distributed throughout the south of Britain. After World Word II Harold Newman of Wales had a show dog named Dewi Sant that was frequently used as a stud. Many Welsh are Dewi's descendants.

In 1952 Miss D. Ellis of England brought a team of five Welsh Springers to show in the United States. These champions served as foundation stock for the breed in this country. Later, Welsh from other British kennels were imported and as a result all American lines of Welsh Springers originated from British lines.

In 1929, the breed was recognized by the American Kennel Club and the official breed standard was adopted.

The Breed Today

Breed Description

The Welsh Springer of today is often mistaken for a Brittany or an English Springer Spaniel of another color by the uninitiated. However, upon close examination it is easy to see they aren't all that similar. Larger and stronger than Cockers, yet smaller than the English Springer, the Welsh is a handy size usually weighing between 35 and 45 pounds (15.7–20.2 kg). Males generally stand approximately 19 inches (50 cm) high and females 18 inches (47 cm). However, it is not unusual to see much larger and smaller individuals within the breed.

The Welsh Springer Spaniel has a distinctive red and white coat.

Though Brittanys, which are now recognized as pointers and not spaniels, can weigh between 30 and 40 pounds (13.5–18 kg) and stand between 17.5 and 20.5 inches (46–52 cm), they have a much leggier appearance than the Welsh. This taller breed can have a dark orange and white or liver and white coat that is either flat or wavy, never silky. Also, they should have light-colored noses of varying degree; black noses disqualify in the show ring. However, Welshies always have red and white coats that should be flat and silky. Most Welshies have dark eyes and noses; hazel eyes and flesh-colored noses are acceptable though as they were seen in the original dogs. And of course, one of the breed's most endearing features are their freckles, lots of freckles.

Heavier and stockier dogs, English Springer Spaniels stand in the 20-inch (51-cm) range and can weigh between 40 and 50 pounds (18–22.5 kg). Coat colors vary, though most people are familiar with the liver and white and black and white. The English has a good deal more feathering than the Welsh. In fact, the Welsh is less fully feathered than many of the other flushing breeds and has a comparatively small ear that gradually narrows toward the tip.

Welsh Springers are still most popular in their native Wales and the western regions of England. Considered a rare breed in the United States (with less than 250 dogs registered with the AKC a year as compared to the English with close to 12,000), Welsh enthusiasts are a devoted group and readily sing the praises of their dogs.

The Welsh Springer as a Hunter

As hunters, Welshies are truly at their best—equally at home on land or in water. Hardy animals, they are able to cover all kinds of terrain. If the breed has a fault, it is that they "excel" as hunters. If not properly trained to work with man as pups, they may well follow their instincts and hunt on their own as adults. Thus, the hunting "team" concept must be ingrained early on.

The Welsh is an endurance dog and should be able to hunt all day easily. Having good bird sense, they are persistent in the field, unafraid of heavy cover, and have natural retrieving ability.

Because they're close-ranging flushing dogs, Welshies usually quarter the field in a businesslike fashion. Oftentimes though, they'll gain a sense for where game might be and elect to forgo quartering in order to head for these areas and look them over.

Aggressive on the bird, the Welsh works fast yet with less flash than the English Springer. Because of their vibrant red and white coats, they are easy to spot while hunting. Spirited animals, Welshies are a joy to watch as they happily perform the work they were bred for.

Unlike English Cockers and English Springers that have split into

The Welsh is a true dual-purpose dog, equally capable of working in the field or competing in the show ring.

show-bred and field-bred varieties, the Welsh Springers are dual-purpose dogs, equally comfortable working in the field or performing in the show ring. Welsh breeders are proud of the fact that their dogs can fill both roles and are committed to keeping them this way.

Personality

Although Welshies easily adapt to any reasonable environment (for example, they may be kept in an apartment if given adequate exercise), they are not content to live as

Extremely devoted to their families, Welsh Springers are not content to live as kennel dogs.

The Devoted Dog

This canine devotion can take extreme proportions. One summer my husband, Lou, and I brought our Welsh, Chelsea, with us on a visit to the shore. We were staying with my folks in their old Victorian house, which boasts a large, wrap-around front porch. After we greeted my father and installed a dog gate to block the stairs, Lou went back to the car to grab our bags.

Surely, Chelsea must have thought he was leaving her. Within moments, she leaped to the top of the railing and sailed nearly nine feet to the ground. Fortunately, thick bushes cushioned her fall. Unharmed, she raced over to Lou wagging her tail.

On another shore visit, my mother decided to take Chelsea for a walk. Only two blocks from the house, she suddenly turned and pulled my mother back home to Lou and I. To this day, my parents tell stories of Chelsea's unusual devotion to us.

Because of their "clingy" natures, some Welshies can become overly dependent on their owners and suffer from separation anxiety when left alone, so it's very important to gradually teach Welsh puppies to accept being by themselves at an early age.

Temperament

As attached as these dogs are to their families, they are not a breed to fawn over strangers. Their attitudes toward those they don't know has been described as reserved, aloof, cautious, and wary.

kennel dogs. Highly people-oriented, these devoted spaniels want to be with their families. They love to be in the middle of activity. Totally loyal to their person, Welshies will follow their owners from room to room, overseeing household chores or listening halfheartedly to telephone conversations. No matter what their beloved person is doing, the Welsh needs to be nearby. No living areas are off-limits. Many are inclined to accompany their owners into the bathroom, often leaning protectively on the shower door or poking their heads past the shower curtain. More than one Welsh owner has been tickled on the lower leg by an inquisitive nose!

Some families expect them to greet guests, but Welshies often hang back to observe a new person. They want to be approached on their own terms. That is, the dog does the greeting, not the other way around. However, once visitors are accepted as friends, Welshies will warm up to them. In fact, they hate being excluded from parties or other social gatherings and will loudly protest if banished from family festivities.

Welsh Springers tend to be homebodies. They like to be close to home and don't have a tendency to wander. Once when the gate to our enclosed yard blew open, Smokey, our Field Spaniel, took off to explore the neighborhood. Chelsea sat on the deck barking anxiously, alerting us to the situation.

Not surprisingly, Welshies are protective of their homes and make fine watchdogs, readily sounding an alarm. However, they are not aggressive and would not be classified as a guard dog. Generally, they are great about warning but seldom snarl or bite.

Yet, at least one Welsh has proven her worth as a protector when the situation warranted it. Catie came to the rescue of her owner when an intruder invaded their home. When she spotted him, she jumped up snapping and snarling. He tried to swing at her, but she was able to run in and bite his legs. She stayed positioned between the would-be robber and her owner, eventually driving him from the house. Catie's proud owner always felt safe with her devoted Welsh nearby.

The Welsh Springer makes an ideal family pet for those who enjoy the company of a very devoted dog. Their medium size lends itself well to household life. They are exceptionally patient with children when raised with them. However, because they will eagerly become involved in their play, they may be too exuberant for families with toddlers. When unaccustomed to living with children, they may be fearful of them. So training and socialization is crucial for those owners who don't have children in order to keep dogs accustomed to youngsters and quick action.

Welsh puppies have an exuberant zest for life—they live their puppyhood to the limit. They can be terrors, hole diggers, and picky eaters. They get in trouble within moments,

Welsh puppies have an exuberant zest for life.

are shy one day and extroverted the next. Just about the time owners wonder when their pups will settle down, at a year to 16 months they begin to blossom into friendly, sweet, loving companions.

Good natured, Welsh Springers generally get along well with other dogs. They do not tend to be aggressive and several dogs can be housed together in harmony. The gentle Welsh is also accepting of different types of animals. When Chelsea joined the family, we owned a rabbit named Domino. Dom hopped over to greet this odd-looking bunny and our young pup took off in the other direction. As she grew, the two became great pals.

We also own a parrot. Chelsea once jumped up on his cage. He swiftly nipped her on the nose. From that day forward, she respected his territory and the two have lived together peacefully for years.

Most Welsh fanciers will say they enjoy the breed's obvious attachment to their owners. But this very trait may be unwelcome by those who don't appreciate such strong canine devotion. Welshies are not dogs for those who are looking for an independent breed content with an occasional good word or game of fetch. These devoted spaniels expect and need to be a part of the family. They are also not a good breed for those who have little patience for the pranks of puppyhood or don't have the time to properly socialize their pups. A Welsh that lives an isolated youth will not mature into a well-balanced adult dog.

Because Welshies have soft temperaments, they also may not be an appropriate choice for strong obedience competitors who are accustomed to tougher-minded breeds. The Welsh's propensity for barking can also be a problem if not properly channeled.

Training

Welsh Springers are an intelligent but slow-to-mature breed. They want to please their people, but some days they'd rather please themselves just a little bit more. They have been described as a "tad stubborn" and "singleminded." Generally speaking, they cannot be

The gentle Welshie tends to be accepting of different types of animals.

Athletic and agile, this Welshman vaults over a jump.

forced to do anything. So it's better to teach good habits using consistent positive training techniques at an early age than to try to correct negative behavior later on. Welshies carry early lessons with them—both good and bad. Catie, who came to the rescue of her owner during a botched burglary, once saw a cat run through a hole in the backyard fence. Every day from that day forward she would go to that hole in the fence every single time she was let outside.

Training Methods

Welshies are neat dogs both in taking care of themselves and in house manners, so they are relatively easy to housebreak. Whether training for the home or obedience ring, it's best to remember Welshies have soft temperaments. Their feelings are easily hurt if owners use harsh words or methods. A negative experience will be remembered for a long time and undermine trust in the owner. Heavy-handed training will do nothing but sabotage the trainer's efforts to have a well-behaved, well-adjusted dog.

In competition training, Welshies do not thrive on repetition. They become disenchanted and even disheartened by drilling something over and over again. They are very, very in tune with their owner's emotions. If their person is nervous, upset, or irritated about something, they will mirror these negative feelings.

Summing up, Welsh Springers perform best with short, diverse training sessions. They will respond to a firm but gentle hand.

Obedience and Agility Trials

Welsh Springer Spaniels are an easy breed to owner-handle in the show ring particularly because their numbers are low and there are few professional handlers in the breed. Because they are intelligent dogs with a basic desire to please, with proper training they can successfully compete in obedience. Athletic and agile, they are great candidates for agility. They also enjoy the thrill of tracking and hunting tests—natural endeavors for this ancient sporting spaniel.

Exercise and Grooming

Unlike many dogs bred to hunt, the Welsh doesn't require a great deal of exercise. Older puppies are an exception and benefit from regular outdoor activity. Because of their boundless energy, long walks and free runs in safe, enclosed areas use up their energy in a constructive manner.

Adult Welsh Springers should be taken on routine walks and have an opportunity to run and play. However, they will not become hyperactive if owners let the exercise regimen slide from time to time.

Coat

It's fairly easy to keep Welsh Springers well groomed. They have a self-cleaning coat; dirt just falls off when it drys. As an added bonus they do not have an offensive doggy odor.

Pets should be brushed and combed once or twice a week. Although the Welsh's body should never be clipped, every six weeks or so ears can be shaved with a number-ten blade with the grain on the top one-third of the ear. The throat can also be shaved with the same blade to about one inch above the breastbone. Trimming the sides of the neck will blend in the shaved area with normal growth. The tail can be neatened and the hair around the paws and between the pads clipped. Show dogs will probably require more frequent attention, and all Welshies should have the hair under the earflap removed to promote air circulation and prevent ear infections.

Breed-Specific Health Concerns

Welsh Springers are hardy dogs with an average life span of 12 to 14 years, though individual dogs have reached the ripe old age of 16 or 17. Although the Welsh has a smaller ear than many of its cousins, infections do occur. Twice-weekly ear maintenance should help ward off the growth of yeast or bacteria.

Many Welsh Springers are sensitive to flea bites and may develop flea allergies. Other disorders known to occur in the breed are hip displa-

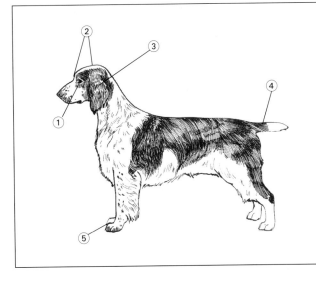

① Oval eye
② Slightly domed skull with moderate stop
③ Low-set, somewhat short ears
④ Docked tail carried near horizontal
⑤ Round feet

❏ **Color:** rich red and white
❏ **DQ:** none

sia, epilepsy, hypothyroidism, and eye problems, including glaucoma, cataracts, and entropion.

Official Standard

General Appearance

The Welsh Springer Spaniel is a dog of distinct variety and ancient origin, who derives his name from his hunting style and not his relationship to other breeds. He is an attractive dog of handy size, exhibiting substance without coarseness. He is compact, not leggy, obviously built for hard work and endurance. The Welsh Springer Spaniel gives the impression of length due to obliquely angled forequarters and well developed hindquarters. Being a hunting dog, he should be shown in hard muscled working condition. His coat should not be so excessive as to hinder his work as an active flushing spaniel, but should be thick enough to protect him from heavy cover and weather.

Size, Proportion, Substance

A dog is ideally 18–19 inches in height at the withers and a bitch is 17–18 inches at the withers. Any animal above or below the ideal to be proportionately penalized. Weight should be in proportion to height and overall balance. Length of body from the withers to the base of the tail is very slightly greater than the distance from the withers to the ground. This body length may be the same as the height but never shorter, thus preserving the rectangular silhouette of the Welsh Springer Spaniel.

Head

The Welsh Springer Spaniel head is unique and should in no way

Three generations of Welsh Springers, mother, daughter, and granddaughter.

approximate that of other spaniel breeds. Its overall balance is of primary importance. Head is in proportion to body, never so broad as to appear coarse nor so narrow as to appear racy. The skull is of medium length, slightly domed, with a clearly defined stop. It is well chiseled below the eyes. The top plane of the skull is very slightly divergent from that of the muzzle, but with no tendency toward a down-faced appearance. A short chubby head is most objectionable. Eyes should be oval in shape, dark to medium brown in color with a soft expression. Preference is for a darker eye though lighter shades of brown are acceptable. Yellow or mean-looking eyes are to be heavily penalized. Medium in size, they are neither prominent, nor sunken, nor do they show haw. Eye rims are tight and dark pigmentation is preferred. Ears arc set on approximately at eye level and hang close to the cheeks. Comparatively small, the leather does not

reach to the nose. Gradually narrowing toward the tip, they are shaped somewhat like a vine leaf and are lightly feathered.

The length of the muzzle is approximately equal to, but never longer than that of the skull. It is straight, fairly square, and free from excessive flew. Nostrils are well developed and black or any shade of brown in color. A pink nose is to be severely penalized. A scissors bite is preferred. An undershot jaw is to be severely penalized.

Neck, Topline, Body

The neck is long and slightly arched, clean in throat, and set into long, sloping shoulders. Topline is level. The loin is slightly arched, muscular, and close-coupled. The croup is very slightly rounded, never steep nor falling off. The topline in combination with proper angulation fore and aft presents a silhouette that appears rectangular. The chest is well developed and muscular with a prominent forechest, the ribs well sprung and the brisket reaching to the elbows. The tail is an extension of the topline. Carriage is nearly horizontal or slightly elevated when the dog is excited. The tail is generally docked and displays a lively action.

Forequarters

The shoulder blade and upper arm are approximately equal in length. The upper arm is set well back, joining the shoulder blade with sufficient angulation to place the elbow beneath the highest point of the shoulder blade when standing. The forearms are of medium length, straight and moderately feathered. The legs are well boned but not to the extent of coarseness. The Welsh Springer Spaniel's elbows should be close to the body and its pasterns short and slightly sloping. Height to the elbows is approximately equal to the distance from the elbows to the top of the shoulder blades. Dewclaws are generally removed. Feet should be round, tight and well arched with thick pads.

Hindquarters

The hindquarters must be strong, muscular, and well boned, but not coarse. When viewed in profile the thighs should be wide and the second thighs well developed. The angulation of the pelvis and femur corresponds to that of the shoulder and upper arm. Bend of stifle is moderate. The bones from the hocks to the pads are short with a well angulated hock joint. When viewed from the side or rear they are perpendicular to the ground. Rear dewclaws are removed. Feet as in front.

Coat

The coat is naturally straight flat and soft to the touch, never wiry or wavy. It is sufficiently dense to be waterproof, thornproof, and weatherproof. The back of the forelegs, the hind legs above the hocks, chest and underside of the body are moderately feathered. The ears and tail are lightly feathered. Coat so excessive as to be a hindrance in the field is to be discouraged. Obvious barbering is to be avoided as well.

Color

The color is rich red and white only. Any pattern is acceptable and any white area may be flecked with red ticking.

Gait

The Welsh Springer moves with a smooth, powerful, ground covering action that displays drive from the rear. Viewed from the side, he exhibits a strong forward stride with a reach that does not waste energy. When viewed from the front, the legs should appear to move forward in an effortless manner with no tendency for the feet to cross over or interfere with each other. Viewed from the rear, the hocks should follow on a line with the forelegs, neither too widely nor too closely spaced. As the speed increases the feet tend to converge towards a center line.

Temperament

The Welsh Springer Spaniel is an active dog displaying a loyal and affectionate disposition. Although reserved with strangers, he is not timid, shy nor unfriendly. To this day he remains a devoted family member and hunting companion.

Approved: June 13, 1989
Effective: August 1, 1989
© 1999 by the American Kennel Club.
Courtesy of the Welsh Springer
Spaniel Club of America

American Water Spaniel

A Cocker pup and pal.

Clumber Spaniel

Future hunters.

English Springer Spaniel

Irish Water Spaniel

English Cocker Spaniel

Sussex Spaniel

Useful Addresses and Literature

Books

Coile, D. Caroline. *Encyclopedia of Dog Breeds.* Barron's Educational Series, Inc., Hauppauge, NY: 1998.

Ditto, Tanya. *English Springer Spaniels: A Complete Pet Owner's Manual.* Barron's Educational Series, Inc., Hauppauge, NY: 1994.

Sucher, Jaime J. *Cocker Spaniels: A Complete Pet Owner's Manual.* Barron's Educational Series, Inc., Hauppauge, NY: 1999.

Ullmann, Hans J., and Evamaria Ullmann. *Spaniels: A Complete Pet Owner's Manual.* Barron's Educational Series, Inc., Hauppauge, NY: 1982.

Magazines and Newsletters

The Dog Love Letter
Dedicated to natural health and healing for dogs.
Telephone: 1-800-580-3644
www.thedogloveletter.com

Dr. Bob & Susan Goldstein's Love of Animals
Natural care and healing for your pets.
Telephone: 1-800-711-2292

Gun Dog
The Stover Publishing Co., Inc.
P.O. Box 35098
Des Moines, IA 50315
Telephone: (515) 243-2472

Natural Dog: Your Complete Guide to Holistic Dog Care
Fancy Publications
An annual publication available on newsstands and in large pet supply stores.

Spaniels in the Field
5312 Wolf Knoll
Orr, MN 55771-8337
Telephone: (218) 343-6253

The Whole Dog Journal
Telephone: 1-800-829-9165
customer_service@belvoir.com

Catalogs

Dogwise
Formerly *The Dog & Cat Book Catalog*
Direct Book Service
Telephone: 1-800-776-2665
www.dogwise.com
E-mail: dgctbook@cascade.net

Morrills's New Directions
A natural pet care catalog.
21 Market Square
Houlton, ME 04730
Telephone: 1-800-368-5057
(In ME, call 1-800-649-0744)

A smiling Welsh Springer pup.

PetSage
Natural medicines, alternative therapies, and specialty products designed for your pet's health and safety.
Telephone: 1-800-738-4584
www.petsage.com
E-mail: info@petsage.com

Whiskers
Organic/raw food diets, vitamins/minerals, herbs, flower/animal essences, books, tapes, videos, and more.
Telephone: 1-800-WHISKERS

Organizations

American Holistic Veterinary Medical Association (AHVMA)
2214 Old Emmorton Road
Bel Air, MD 21015
Telephone: (410) 569-0795
Fax: (410) 515-7774

The American Kennel Club (AKC)
5580 Centerview Drive, Suite 200
Raleigh, NC 27606
Telephone: (919) 233-9767

The American Veterinary Medical Association (AVMA)
1931 North Meacham Road, Suite 100
Schaumburg, IL 60173-4360
Telephone: (847) 925-8070

Veterinary Pet Insurance
Telephone: 1-800-872-7387
www.petinsurance.com
E-mail: usapets@primenet.com

National Sporting Spaniel Parent Clubs

American Spaniel Club, Inc. (Cocker Spaniels)

The American Water Spaniel Club, Inc.

The Clumber Spaniel Club of America

The English Cocker Spaniel Club of America, Inc.

English Springer Spaniel Field Trial Association, Inc.

Field Spaniel Society of America

The Irish Water Spaniel Club of America

Sussex Spaniel Club of America, Inc.

Welsh Springer Spaniel Club of America

To locate current club secretaries, contact the American Kennel Club at:
5580 Centerview Drive, Suite 200
Raleigh, NC 27606
Telephone: (919) 233-9767

Index